Discovering Literature Series

A Teaching Guide to

Mrs. Frisby and the Rats of NIMH

by Mary F. Spicer

Illustration by Kathy Kifer and Dahna Solar

Dedicated to
Wendel Z. (Sam) Hall
1938-1994
A teacher's teacher—always a source of inspiration
and encouragement to me.

Mrs. Frisby and the Rats of NIMH
Aladdin Paperbacks
An imprint of Simon & Schuster Children's Publishing Division
New York, New York 10020

Published by:
Garlic Press
100 Hillview Lane #2
Eugene, OR 97408

ISBN 0-931993-78-4
Order Number GP-078

Table of Contents

Notes to the Teacher 5
    About Chapter Organization 5
    About the Skill Pages 7
    About the Tests 7
    About the Writer's Forum 7

Chapter 1   The Sickness of Timothy Frisby 8
Chapter 2   Mr. Ages 9
Chapter 3   The Crow and the Cat 10
    •Skill Page: Writing Fantasy 11
Chapter 4   Mr. Fitzgibbon's Plow 12
Chapter 5   Five Days 13
    •Test: Chapters 1-5 14

Chapter 6   A Favor from Jeremy 17
Chapter 7   The Owl 18
Chapter 8   "Go to the Rats" 19
Chapter 9   In the Rosebush 20
    •Skill Page: Elements of a Narrative 21
Chapter 10 Brutus 23
    •Skill Page: About the Characters 24
    •Test: Chapters 6-10 25

Chapter 11 In the Library 28
Chapter 12 Isabella 29
    •Skill Page: Sequencing 30
Chapter 13 A Powder for Dragon 31
Chapter 14 The Marketplace 32
    •Skill Page: Cause and Effect 33
Chapter 15 In the Cage 34
    •Test: Chapters 11-15 35

Chapter 16 The Maze 38
Chapter 17 A Lesson in Reading.. 39
   •Skill Page: The Lab at NIMH 40
Chapter 18 The Air Ducts.. 42
Chapter 19 The Boniface Estate 43
Chapter 20 The Main Hall 44
   •Skill Page: About the Characters, Part 2 45
   •Test: Chapters 16-20 46

Chapter 21 The Toy Tinker.. 49
Chapter 22 Thorn Valley 50
   •Skill Page: Outlining 51
Chapter 23 Captured 54
Chapter 24 Seven Dead Rats 55
   •Writer's Forum: Newspaper Writing 56
Chapter 25 Escape 58
   •Writer's Forum: Explaining Information...................... 59
   •Test: Chapters 21-25 60

Chapter 26 At the Meeting 63
Chapter 27 The Doctor 64
   •Skill Page: Character Development 65
Chapter 28 Epilogue 68
   •Skill Page: Plot Development 69
   •Test: Chapters 26-28 71

Chapter Summary & Vocabulary (Blackline Master) 74

Sample Cover Sheet 75

Answer Pages 76

The Discovering Literature Series is designed to develop a student's appreciation for good literature and to improve reading comprehension. While many skills reinforce a student's ability to comprehend what he or she reads (sequencing, cause and effect, finding details, using context clues), two skills are vital. They are: discerning **main ideas** and **summarizing** text. Students who can master these two essential skills develop into sophisticated readers.

The following discussion details the various elements that structure this Series.

About Chapter Organization

Sample: Chapter 2
with Student Directives,
Chapter Vocabulary, and
Chapter Summary

Each chapter analysis is organized into three basic elements: **Student Directives**, **Chapter Vocabulary**, and **Chapter Summary**. Student Directives and Chapter Vocabulary need to be displayed on the board or on an overhead projector after each chapter is read. Students copy the Chapter Vocabulary and write their own summaries following the Student Directives.

The **Student Directives** contain the main ideas in each chapter. They provide the students, working individually or in groups, with a framework for developing their summaries. Student Directives can also be used as group discussion topics.

The **Chapter Vocabulary** includes definitions of key words from each chapter. To save time, students need only to copy, not look up, definitions. Suggestions for teaching vocabulary to students are as follows:

1. Make and display flashcards with the words and definitions. Refer to vocabulary cards in daily review.
2. Have students write sentences individually, in groups, or as a class using the words in the story's context.
3. Give frequent quizzes before an actual test.
4. Have students make their own vocabulary crossword puzzles or word search puzzles.
5. Play 20 questions with vocabulary words.
6. Host a vocabulary bee where the students give definitions for the word rather than spelling it.

A **Chapter Summary** for each chapter is included for teacher use and knowledge. Some students may initially need to copy the summaries in order to feel comfortable writing their own subsequent ones. Other students can use the completed summaries as a comparison to guide their own work. Summary

Sample:
Blackline Master

writing provides an opportunity to polish student composition skills, in addition to reading skills.

The **blackline master**, *Chapter Summary & Vocabulary*, is provided on page 74. It can be duplicated for student use. Teachers can also use it to make transparencies for displaying Student Directives and Chapter Vocabulary.

In addition, teachers may opt to have students make folders to house their Chapter Summary & Vocabulary sheets. A sample cover sheet (see page 75) for student embellishments has been provided. Cover sheets can be laminated, if desired, and affixed to a manila (or other) folder.

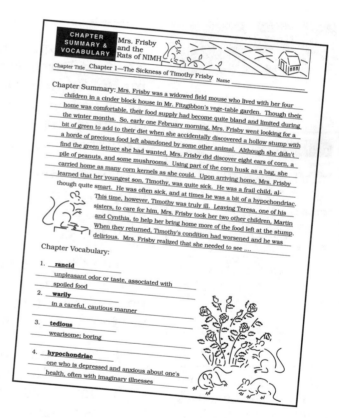

Sample Transparency:
Student Directives and Chapter Vocabulary

Sample Transparency:
Chapter Summary and Chapter Vocabulary

The above two samples serve to illustrate how the **blackline master**, *Chapter Summary & Vocabulary*, can be used as a transparency to focus student work. These transparencies are particularly effective for displaying Student Directives and Chapter Vocabulary. They are also effective for initially modeling how Chapter Summaries can be written.

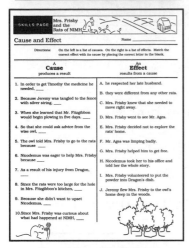

Sample: Skill Page

Skill Pages throughout the series have been developed to increase students' understanding of various literary elements and to reinforce vital reading skills. Since the entire series is devoted to reinforcing **main ideas** and **summarizing** skills, no further work has been provided on these skills. Depending upon each novel, Skill Pages reinforce various skills from among the following: **outlining**; **cause and effect**; **sequencing**; **character**, **setting**, **and plot development**; and **figurative language**. You will note that character development is based upon a values framework.

About the
Tests

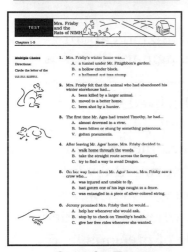

Sample: Test

At the end of each five-chapter block, a comprehensive open-book **Test** has been developed for your use. Each test includes reading comprehension, vocabulary, and short essays.

An Answer Key is provided at the back of the book for each Test.

The vocabulary portion of the Tests may be particularly difficult. You will probably want to give one or two vocabulary quizzes before administering each of the six Tests.

About the
Writer's Forum

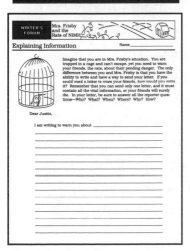

Sample: Writer's Forum

Suggestions for writing are presented under the **Writer's Forum** throughout this guide. You can choose from these suggestions or substitute your own creative-writing ideas.

"The Sickness of Timothy Frisby"

Student Directives

1. Briefly discuss Mrs. Frisby, her family, and home.

2. Review the treasure Mrs. Frisby discovered.

3. Briefly describe Timothy and his illness.

4. Tell what Mrs. Frisby needed to do to help Timothy.

Vocabulary

rancid	unpleasant odor or taste, associated with spoiled food
warily	in a careful, cautious manner
tedious	wearisome; boring
hypochondriac	one who is depressed and anxious about one's health, often with imaginary illnesses

Summary

Mrs. Frisby was a widowed field mouse who lived with her four children in a cinder block house in Mr. Fitzgibbon's vegetable garden. Though their home was comfortable, their food supply had become quite bland and limited during the winter months. So, early one February morning, Mrs. Frisby went looking for a bit of green to add to their diet when she accidentally discovered a hollow stump with a horde of precious food left abandoned by some other animal. Although she didn't find the green lettuce she had wanted, Mrs. Frisby did discover eight ears of corn, a pile of peanuts, and some mushrooms. Using part of the corn husk as a bag, she carried home as many corn kernels as she could. Upon arriving home, Mrs. Frisby learned that her youngest son, Timothy, was quite sick. He was a frail child, although quite smart. He was often sick, and at times he was a bit of a hypochondriac. This time, however, Timothy was truly ill. Leaving Teresa, one of his sisters, to care for him, Mrs. Frisby took her two other children, Martin and Cynthia, to help her bring home more of the food left at the stump. When they returned, Timothy's condition had worsened and he was delirious. Mrs. Frisby realized that she needed to see Mr. Ages about medicine for her sick son.

"Mr. Ages"

1. Tell about Mrs. Frisby's journey to visit Mr. Ages.

2. Briefly describe Mr. Ages and his home.

3. Discuss Mrs. Frisby's first journey to Mr. Ages' house.

4. Review Mr. Ages' diagnosis of and prescription for Timothy's condition.

cautious   careful; watchful

relentlessly harshly; in a manner showing no pity for others

loped   moved with a long, swinging stride

vigorous   strong; energetic

Summary

Having said good-bye to her children, Mrs. Frisby set out on her journey to Mr. Ages' farmhouse, being careful to avoid the cat and other dangerous enemies. Mr. Ages, a white mouse who lived in a brick wall of a burned-down farmhouse, was very wise and knew a great deal about medicine. Mrs. Frisby had visited Mr. Ages once before while her husband was alive. At that time, they had brought Timothy because he was unconscious after having been stung or bitten. Mr. Ages had diagnosed Timothy's condition as a poisonous spider bite, and he had prescribed a milky liquid. Although the milky liquid cured Timothy, he had never regained his previous good health. This time Mr. Ages asked Mrs. Frisby a series of questions about Timothy's condition and diagnosed pneumonia. He prescribed a powder wrapped in neat white packets, to be administered for three days. Mr. Ages explained that Timothy would improve a bit each day, but he would have to stay completely away from cold air for a month, or he might not recover.

"The Crow and the Cat"

Student Directives

1. Briefly discuss Mrs. Frisby's choice of a route home.

2. Describe Dragon, Mr. Fitzgibbon's cat.

3. Review Mrs. Frisby's meeting with the crow.

4. Discuss how Jeremy saved Mrs. Frisby and his promise to her.

Vocabulary

apt	fitting; suitable; appropriate
invariably	constantly; always uniformly
dubiously	in a doubting or uncertain manner
literally	according to the strict meaning of the words

Summary

As Mrs. Frisby left Mr. Ages, she faced two choices for her trip home—one, walking alone in the dark woods, and the other, cutting straight across the farmyard. Since the forest at night was filled with danger, Mrs. Frisby chose the second route despite her fear of getting caught by Dragon, Mr. Fitzgibbon's cat. Dragon was a fierce hunter with curving fangs and seven claws on each foot. Hopeful that she could spot Dragon in the daylight, Mrs. Frisby proceeded until she came upon a young crow who had become caught on a fence by a length of silver-colored string. Realizing that the crow would never be able to free himself, Mrs. Frisby stopped to offer him assistance, but only after she scolded him for behaving so foolishly. As she worked to free him, the crow spotted Dragon. Thinking quickly, the crow commanded Mrs. Frisby to jump on his back, and off they flew just in time to avoid the screaming, angry cat. The crow, whose name was Jeremy, dropped Mrs. Frisby off at her house and promised to help her whenever she might need him.

Mrs. Frisby
and the
Rats of NIMH

Writing Fantasy

Name _____

Robert C. O'Brien is a highly imaginative writer of children's novels. By teaming his vivid imagination with his ability to write engaging stories, O'Brien has earned awards for excellence in children's literature. In 1972, his novel *Mrs. Frisby and the Rats of NIMH* won both the Newbery Medal and the Lewis Carroll Shelf Award.

When he began to plan *Mrs. Frisby and the Rats of NIMH,* O'Brien chose to develop his story line using a type of literature called fantasy. A play or story that is full of imagination and quite unreal, like *Peter Pan*, is termed "fantasy." In order to write fantasy well, a writer must first conceive an idea that will so involve his or her readers in the story that, for a while at least, they accept the fantasy world as one that is meaningful, one that makes sense. If the author were to reach a point where the fantasy becomes bizarre, then his creation would crumble, and it would no longer be believable to readers. With total mastery of the writing craft, Robert C.O'Brien makes the magic of his fantasy world seem very real to his readers.

Initially, readers must accept the idea that animals, such as mice, rats, and crows, can communicate with each other and work together to solve their problems. In his novel, O'Brien has chosen a group of rats as the unlikely heroes of his story. Only a masterful storyteller could convince readers that rats are the "good guys," yet O'Brien does just that in this classic story.

Not only does O'Brien tell an engaging story, but he also raises his readers' social awareness. Young readers learn the dangers of excessive technology. Also, they learn about the importance of ethics in our technological age. In O'Brien's fantasy world, the heroes always demonstrate a heightened sense of responsibility to their community.

Directions: After carefully reading the above article, match the terms on the left with the phrases on the right. Place the correct letter on each line.

_____ 1. Robert C. O'Brien   A. an imaginative story that is quite unreal

_____ 2. Newbery Medal   B. concern about problems facing society

_____ 3. imagination   C. author of *Mrs. Frisby and the Rats of NIMH*

_____ 4. fantasy   D. animals that communicate in a fantasy

_____ 5. mice, rats, and crows   E. yearly award given for excellent childrens' literature

_____ 6. social awareness   F. rules of right and wrong behavior

_____ 7. ethics   G. making up an idea in one's mind

"Mr. Fitzgibbon's Plow"

Student Directives

1. Describe Timothy's reaction to the medicine.

2. Relate why Moving Day was a problem for Mrs. Frisby.

3. Discuss Mrs. Frisby's meeting with the shrew.

4. Describe what alarmed Mrs. Frisby.

Vocabulary

subdued   quiet; not as active as usual

illogical   contrary to the rules of sound reasoning

Summary

When Mrs. Frisby returned with Timothy's medicine, he was very weak and could hardly talk. The medicine worked as Mr. Ages had predicted, and in a few days, his condition improved. Feeling more cheerful, Mrs. Frisby went for a walk in the spring sunshine. The warm day triggered a nagging worry for Mrs. Frisby—Moving Day, a day when they would have to move out of Mr. Fitzgibbon's garden. Since Mr. Fitzgibbon's tractor plowed through the garden as soon as the weather allowed, all the animals living there had to move to their summer homes. Mrs. Frisby was worried that Timothy would not be well enough to make the move. While walking through the garden, Mrs. Frisby met a shrew who was a friend of hers. The shrew felt that Mr. Fitzgibbon would start plowing soon, and illogically said that she wished someone would plow through his house. Remembering a saying that Mr. Frisby had told her about finding the key to unlock the door, Mrs. Frisby decided to find a solution to her problem. Then she heard the alarming sound of Mr. Fitzgibbon starting his tractor.

"Five Days"

1. Review the conversation Mrs. Frisby overheard between Mr. Fitzgibbon and his sons.

2. Discuss Mrs. Frisby's encounter with Dragon.

3. Briefly describe the activity of the rats.

4. Tell Dragon's reaction to the rats.

respite   a temporary period of relief or rest

vantage   favorable or advantageous position for observing

laboriously   with much labor, toil, or difficulty

Summary

   Mrs. Frisby, deciding to investigate the doings of Mr. Fitzgibbon, hid in a convenient knothole in the fence nearest the tractor shed. She was relieved to learn that plowing would not begin for another five days, but she realized that she still needed to make arrangements for Timothy. Without thinking, Mrs. Frisby carelessly climbed out of the knothole—not ten feet from Dragon. Surprised that he did not attack, Mrs. Frisby quickly scurried away, still wondering what had caused this change in Dragon's behavior. To make the day even odder, Mrs. Frisby saw columns of gray rats hauling a long piece of electric cable through the grass. Quickly, she guessed that they were taking the wire to their rat hole near the rosebush, but she couldn't figure out what they would want with it. All during the rats' maneuvers, Dragon slept on.

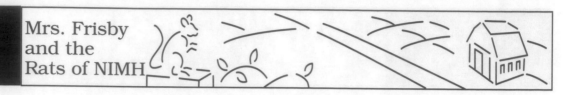

TEST

Mrs. Frisby
and the
Rats of NIMH

Chapters 1-5, Page 1

Name _____

Multiple Choice

Directions:

Circle the letter of the

correct answer.

1. Mrs. Frisby's winter home was...
   A. a tunnel under Mr. Fitzgibbon's garden.
   B. a hollow cinder block.
   C. a hollowed-out tree stump.

2. Mrs. Frisby felt that the animal who had abandoned his winter storehouse had...
   A. been killed by a larger animal.
   B. moved to a better home.
   C. been shot by a hunter.

3. The first time Mr. Ages had treated Timothy, he had...
   A. almost drowned in a river.
   B. been bitten or stung by something poisonous.
   C. gotten pneumonia.

4. After leaving Mr. Ages' home, Mrs. Frisby decided to...
   A. walk home through the woods.
   B. take the straight route across the farmyard.
   C. try to find a way to avoid Dragon.

5. On her way home from Mr. Ages' house, Mrs. Frisby saw a crow who...
   A. was injured and unable to fly.
   B. had gotten one of his legs caught in a fence.
   C. was entangled in a piece of silver-colored string.

6. Jeremy promised Mrs. Frisby that he would...
   A. help her whenever she would ask.
   B. stop by to check on Timothy's health.
   C. give her free rides whenever she wanted.

TEST

Mrs. Frisby
and the
Rats of NIMH

Chapters 1-5, Page 2

Name _____

7. Field mice that lived in gardens during the winter, like Mrs. Frisby, had to move to...

    A. barn lofts during the summer.

    B. eaves and attics during the summer.

    C. fields that were not used for summer crops.

8. Mrs. Frisby learned that Mr. Fitzgibbon would not begin plowing for five days because...

    A. the weather was not warm enough.

    B. the part for the tractor would take five days to come into Henderson's store.

    C. he needed to work on the farm.

9. Dragon surprised Mrs. Frisby when she came out from her knothole hiding place because he...

    A. was ready to pounce on her.

    B. didn't even see her.

    C. didn't take the trouble to get up and chase her.

10. In addition to Dragon, another oddity that disturbed Mrs. Frisby was...

    A. Timothy's miraculous recovery.

    B. a column of rats hauling pieces of outdoor wiring.

    C. a column of rats marching by Dragon.

Vocabulary

Directions:

Fill in the blank with

the correct word.

tedious	vigorous	illogical
hypochondriac	apt	respite
relentlessly	dubiously	laboriously
	subdued	

1. _____ quiet; not as active as usual

2. _____ in a doubting or uncertain manner

3. _____ harshly; in a manner showing no pity for others

TEST

Mrs. Frisby
and the
Rats of NIMH

Chapters 1-5, Page 3

Name _____

4. _____ a temporary period of relief or rest

5. _____ one who is depressed and anxious about one's health, often with an imaginary illness

6. _____ fitting; suitable; appropriate

7. _____ strong; energetic

8. _____ contrary to the rules of sound reasoning

9. _____ wearisome; boring

10. _____ with much labor, toil, or difficulty

Essay Questions

Directions:

Answer in complete

sentences.

1. Timothy Frisby was not as healthy as his brothers and sisters, but he had developed many personal qualities which made him lovable. Describe Timothy's personality, giving examples from the story.

_____

_____

_____

2. When Mrs. Frisby first met Jeremy, she thought he was a "birdbrain" and remembered what her husband used to say: "The size of the brain is no measure of its capacity." What does this statement mean with regard to Jeremy?

_____

_____

_____

3. Why couldn't Mrs. Frisby move Timothy to their summer home?

_____

_____

_____

"A Favor from Jeremy"

Student Directives

1. Discuss Mrs. Frisby's encounter with Jeremy.

2. Tell why Jeremy collected shiny things.

3. Relate Jeremy's suggestion to Mrs. Frisby.

4. Discuss briefly their plans for meeting with the owl.

Vocabulary

essence   fundamental nature of something

plummeted   fell straight downward

Summary

   After worrying about Moving Day and watching the tractor, the cat, and the rats, Mrs. Frisby remembered that she needed to get more corn kernels from the stump. Along the way, she spotted Jeremy the crow, who was busy trying to pick up a piece of tin foil. Mrs. Frisby decided that he might be able to help her with her Moving Day problem, and she ran over to meet him. Mrs. Frisby discovered that Jeremy had a girlfriend who was very fond of shiny things that sparkled in the sun. After Mrs. Frisby explained her problem about Timothy and Moving Day, Jeremy suggested that she seek the advice of the wise owl who lived in a large beech tree deep in the forest. Whenever the crows or other birds had a problem, they always consulted with the owl. Since Mrs. Frisby couldn't have found her way alone, Jeremy agreed to pick her up at dusk, which was the best time to speak to the owl.

"The Owl"

Student Directives

1. Discuss Jeremy's introduction to Mrs. Frisby's children.

2. Briefly describe their flight to the owl's house.

3. Review Mrs. Frisby's and the owl's reactions to meeting each other.

Vocabulary

expedition	a journey for some definite purpose
primeval	ancient; primitive
instinctively	by natural impulse
perceive	to become aware of

Summary

Just as he had promised, Jeremy came by to pick up Mrs. Frisby at five o'clock where she was waiting with her children. Cynthia was afraid of Jeremy, but Martin wished that he was the one making the trip. Trying hard to hide her terror, Mrs. Frisby climbed on Jeremy's back and pressed her face against his feathers. Once they were airborne, Mrs. Frisby realized how different her world appeared from the air. After a while they arrived at the gloomy, primeval forest where the owl lived. Jeremy introduced Mrs. Frisby to the owl, who had trouble believing that a crow would befriend a mouse. Upon hearing Jeremy's dramatic rescue from Dragon, the owl invited Mrs. Frisby into his home to discuss her problem. At first, Mrs. Frisby was afraid of the owl, but Jeremy persuaded her that the owl would not harm her.

"'Go to the Rats'"

1. Discuss the owl's initial advice to Mrs. Frisby.

2. Relate why the owl's manner changed toward Mrs. Frisby.

3. Review the owl's new suggestion to Mrs. Frisby.

4. Discuss Jeremy's meaning for "into the lee."

5. Briefly discuss Jeremy's reaction to the owl's suggestion.

Vocabulary

feasible	possible; practicable; workable
agitated	disturbed; excited; flustered
deference	courteous regard or respect
sentry	military guard posted to give warning

Summary

At Mrs. Frisby's meeting with the owl, the owl was polite but seemed disinterested in solving her problem. Convinced that the owl could offer her no solution, Mrs. Frisby sadly prepared to return home. When the owl asked her to repeat her name, he realized that she was the widow of Jonathan Frisby, a highly respected mouse. Offering Mrs. Frisby some top-secret advice, the owl explained that the rats she had seen marching on the Fitzgibbon farm might be able to help her move her cinder block house. The owl advised Mrs. Frisby to locate the rosebush opening to the rats' home. There she would find a door guarded by a sentry named Justin, and she was to request a meeting with a rat named Nicodemus. Because the owl had been sworn to secrecy by the rats, he was unable to reveal the nature of their projects, but he was sure the rats would help her. As he prepared for his nightly travels, the owl advised her to tell the rats to move her house "into the lee of the stone." After Mrs. Frisby had climbed on Jeremy's back for the return flight, Jeremy explained that "into the lee" meant on "the calm side, the side the wind doesn't blow from." Jeremy agreed with the owl's suggestion to seek assistance from the rats.

"In the Rosebush"

Student Directives

1. Discuss Mrs. Frisby's return home.

2. Review Mrs. Frisby's talk with Timothy.

3. Briefly describe the entrance to the rats' home.

4. Tell what Mrs. Frisby saw at the entrance.

Vocabulary

domain	territory; the land controlled by someone or by a group
dense	thick; closely packed
timidly	in a fearful manner

Summary

Mrs. Frisby returned home to three worried children who were happy about her return. After asking about Timothy's health, Mrs. Frisby went in to see him. She was surprised to find him sitting up in bed, thinking about Moving Day. Even though Timothy realized the danger he was in, he calmly reassured his mother that he wanted to move to their summer home. Not wanting to tell Timothy about the owl's advice in case nothing could be done, Mrs. Frisby merely asked Timothy not to worry about Moving Day. The next morning Mrs. Frisby set out for the large, dense rosebush where she searched for an opening to the rats' home. She entered through a dark tunnel which led to a large clearing about five feet across. Sunlight filtered through the mossy cave at the end of which was a neatly lined stone entrance. And beside the entranceway was the largest rat she had ever seen.

Elements of a Narrative

When an author creates a novel, a movie, or a television script, he or she must carefully plan a story which includes three basic elements: characters, setting, and plot. Simply stated, *somebody* has to be *somewhere* doing *something*. The author's story has merit if the characters are believable, engaging, and well developed. The setting(s) must be accurately described so that the reader can create a mental picture of it in his or her own mind. Specific details are vital in the development of a narrative; details make the story "come alive" for the reader.

Possibly the most complex narrative element is the plot. To develop the plot, the author must carefully plan a sequence of events which will hold the reader's or viewer's interest throughout the book, movie, or TV show. The author must concentrate on only the important aspects of the story so that it doesn't drag on endlessly. Additionally, the events must present a problem which the central character must resolve—either happily or unhappily.

Throughout the introductory chapters or scenes, the author must make the elements of characters, setting, and plot clear to the reader or viewer. Using the introductory chapters as a guide, complete the following "Elements of a Narrative Outline" from *Mrs. Frisby and the Rats of NIMH.*

Mrs. Frisby
and the
Rats of NIMH

Elements of a Narrative Outline

Name_____

Directions: Analyze the three basic elements of a narrative from your reading thus far in *Mrs. Frisby and the Rats of NIMH.* Complete the following outline for your analysis.

Main Character *(somebody)* Describe the mouse introduced in the first chapter.

A. _____

_____

B. _____

_____

C. _____

_____

Setting *(somewhere)* Describe the setting where the story unfolds.

A. Where: _____

_____

B. When: _____

_____

Plot *(something)*
series

From your reading so far, describe how the plot (as a of events) has be developed.

A. _____

_____

B. _____

_____

C. _____

_____

D. _____

_____

"Brutus"

1. Discuss Brutus' reaction to Mrs. Frisby.

2. Review Mrs. Frisby's chance meeting with Mr. Ages.

3. Tell about Mr. Ages' connection with the rats.

4. Discuss the meeting with Justin.

Vocabulary

cordial   friendly, courteous; sincere; warm

doubtful   uncertain; not sure of the truth of a matter

adjourned   to put off until another date or time

Summary

The large, muscular rat standing guard at the entrance to the rats' home treated Mrs. Frisby rudely and asked her to leave. The rat's name was Brutus, and he was substituting for Justin, who was attending a meeting. Sadly, Mrs. Frisby turned away, wondering what she could do next. Listening carefully, Mrs. Frisby heard a frightening, scraping noise approaching the entrance to the rosebush and was relieved to see that it was Mr. Ages. He had broken his ankle and was limping badly. Mrs. Frisby told Mr. Ages her whole story and her problem with Moving Day. She was surprised to learn that Mr. Ages was well acquainted with the rats, and like the owl, he too was sworn to secrecy. As Mrs. Frisby and Mr. Ages approached the entrance again, they noticed that another rat had joined Brutus at his post; this was the rat named Justin. Mr. Ages introduced Mrs. Frisby to the two rats, with Justin noting her last name and realizing that she was Jonathan Frisby's widow. Like the owl, Justin respected Mrs. Frisby's late husband, and he bowed politely to her. Brutus, realizing his error, apologized for his rudeness. Once the introductions had ended, Mr. Ages requested a meeting with Nicodemus.

Mrs. Frisby and the Rats of NIMH

About the Characters

Name _____

Directions: Below is a Character Chart to help you organize the characters from the novel. Fill in whatever information is missing—either the character's name or a character summary. Use this list of characters for the Character Chart.

Mrs. Frisby	Martin	Jeremy	Dragon	Jonathan Frisby
Timothy	Teresa	the owl	Justin	the shrew
Cynthia	Mr. Ages	Brutus	Mr. Fitzgibbon	

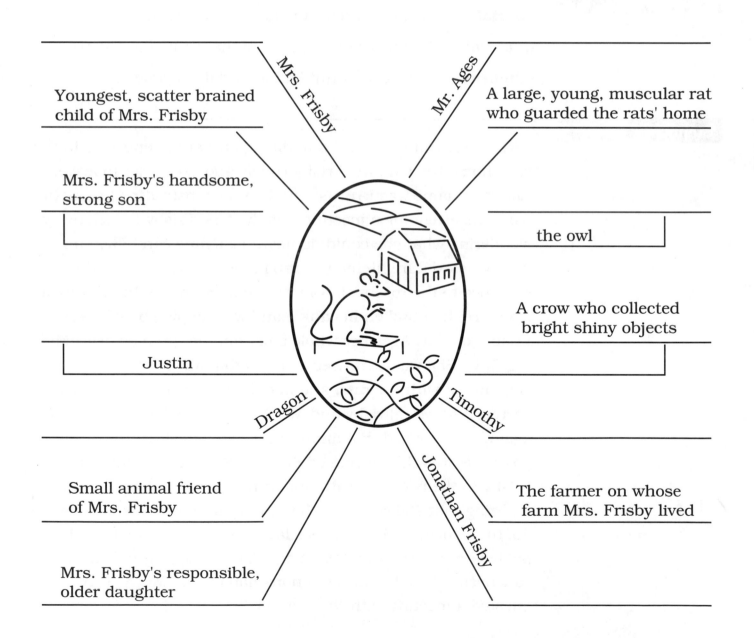

Youngest, scatter brained child of Mrs. Frisby

Mrs. Frisby

Mr. Ages

A large, young, muscular rat who guarded the rats' home

Mrs. Frisby's handsome, strong son

the owl

A crow who collected bright shiny objects

Justin

Small animal friend of Mrs. Frisby

Dragon

Timothy

Jonathan Frisby

The farmer on whose farm Mrs. Frisby lived

Mrs. Frisby's responsible, older daughter

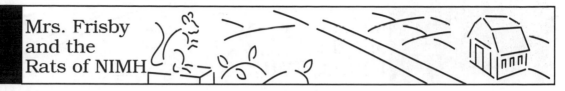
Multiple Choice

Directions:

Circle the letter of the

correct answer.

1. When Mrs. Frisby saw Jeremy trying to pick up shiny
   pieces of foil, she learned that Jeremy...
   A. had a collection of shiny material.
   B. was going to use it to line his nest.
   C. had a girlfriend.

2. When Mrs. Frisby told Jeremy about Moving Day and Timo-
   thy, Jeremy suggested that she...
   A. go back to see Mr. Ages.
   B. go to see the wise old owl.
   C. ask the rats for help.

3. When the wise old owl invited Mrs. Frisby into his home,
   she was...
   A. happy because she thought he would offer good advice.
   B. frightened because owls sometimes eat mice.
   C. worried that Jeremy might fly away and leave her.

4. The owl told Mrs. Frisby about the rats only after he learned that...
   A. she saved Jeremy's life.
   B. she knew Mr. Ages.
   C. she was Jonathan Frisby's widow.

5. With regard to Jonathan Frisby, the owl obviously felt that
   Jonathan had been...
   A. a highly respected mouse.
   B. a close personal friend of Jeremy.
   C. the leader of the owls.

6. The owl behaved strangely when talking about the rats
   because...
   A. he was afraid of them.
   B. the rats did not like the owl.
   C. he was sworn to secrecy about their project.

TEST

Mrs. Frisby
and the
Rats of NIMH

Chapters 6-10, Page 2

Name _____

7. With regard to Mrs. Frisby's house, the owl suggested moving it...

    A. to a location near the rats' home.

    B. into the lee of the stone.

    C. deep into the woods.

8. When Mrs. Frisby arrived home after her visit to the owl, Timothy...

    A. reassured her that he wanted to move to their summer home.

    B. told her that he was feeling much stronger.

    C. asked for some of the corn kernels and peanuts.

9. When Mrs. Frisby first introduced herself to Brutus, he...

    A. invited her into the rats' entranceway.

    B. asked her to wait until Justin arrived.

    C. told her to go away.

10. Mrs. Frisby would not have been able to enter the rats' home had it not been for...

    A. Jeremy pleading with the rats.

    B. Mrs. Frisby telling the rats about meeting with the owl.

    C. a proper introduction from Mr. Ages.

Vocabulary

Directions:

Fill in the blank with

the correct word.

plummeted	feasible	timidly
expedition	agitated	cordial
perceive	sentry	doubtful
	domain	

1. _____   possible; practicable; workable

2. _____   friendly, courteous; sincere; warm

3. _____   territory; the land controlled by someone or by a group

4. _____   to identify with difficulty; observe

5. _____   fell straight downward

6. _____   disturbed; excited; flustered

7. _____   in a fearful manner

8. _____   a journey for some definite purpose

9. _____   uncertain; unsure

10. _____   military guard posted to give warning

Essay Questions

Directions:

Answer in complete

sentences.

1. When Mrs. Frisby first met the owl and Brutus, they were inclined to ignore her request for help. Only when they learned that her last name was Frisby did they agree to help her. Why did both the owl and Brutus change after hearing her last name?

   _____

   _____

   _____

   _____

2. Robert C. O'Brien makes the characters of both Timothy Frisby and his brother Martin seem very real to his readers. Contrast Timothy's personality with Martin's, giving examples from the novel.

   _____

   _____

   _____

   _____

   _____

"In the Library"

Student Directives

1. Briefly discuss Mrs. Frisby's underground walk.

2. Describe the rats' modern conveniences.

3. Describe Nicodemus and his introduction to Mrs. Frisby.

5. Discuss Mrs. Frisby's stay in the rats' library.

5. Tell about the printing on the blackboard.

Vocabulary

detect	to discover the presence of
radiated	spread out from the center, as in rays
hostile	unfriendly, like an enemy; warlike
dredged	searched deeply to bring to the surface

Summary

Mrs. Frisby, Mr. Ages, and Justin walked down a long tunnel in total darkness. After the blackout, Mrs. Frisby detected the faint glow of light which led to a long, carpeted, well-lit hallway. Electricity was only one of the modern conveniences the rats had. Their lights were small Christmas tree bulbs, recessed into the walls and ceiling and covered with glass. Fresh, clean air circulated even though they were three feet underground. Because Mr. Ages was limping badly, the trio used the elevator, causing Mrs. Frisby to gasp, since she had never ridden on an elevator. After the ride, Mrs. Frisby saw a series of rooms, one of which was a large assembly room with many rats talking, standing, and scurrying about. Surprised to see a stranger in their midst, many rats briefly stared at her, but they did not seem hostile. A lean, dignified rat with a scarred face and a black patch over one eye walked toward them and was introduced as Nicodemus. Nicodemus also spoke respectfully of her late husband and promised to help if he could. Since the rats' meeting was about to begin, Mrs. Frisby was taken to the library where a blackboard with large letters read: THE PLAN OF THE RATS OF NIMH.

"Isabella"

1. Discuss Mrs. Frisby's interest in the rats' Plan.

2. Describe Mrs. Frisby's meeting with Isabella.

3. Tell what Mrs. Frisby learned from Isabella.

explicit	plain or clear in language; definite
incomprehensible	not understandable; unintelligible
irrelevantly	in a manner not relating to the subject
apparent	visible; readily understood; obvious

Summary

   Mrs. Frisby was becoming increasingly more curious about the rats' colony. She wondered about the Plan, about the nature of NIMH, and about the rats. Looking down the hall, she was curious about the other rooms, but decided not to investigate since Nicodemus had explicitly asked her to wait in the library. Mrs. Frisby stared at a schedule which had been written on the blackboard, but it was incomprehensible to her. While puzzling over it, a young girl-rat entered the library and was startled to see Mrs. Frisby there. After questioning Mrs. Frisby and realizing that she was not a spy, the girl-rat introduced herself as Isabella. Mrs. Frisby learned that Isabella was romantically interested in Justin, but she was too young at present for marriage. Mrs. Frisby also learned a great deal about the rats' colony. She learned that the rats had a grain room and that the female rats sometimes went to meetings and sometimes not. Nicodemus appeared to be their leader. There was a Plan for the future that some rats did not like, and that one rat, named Jenner, had deserted. She could have learned more but Nicodemus, Justin, Mr. Ages, and another rat, a stranger, entered the library.

Sequencing

Name _____

Event 1: _____
_____

Event 2: Mr. Ages prescribes medicine.
_____

Event 3: _____
_____

Event 4: _____
_____

Event 5: Mrs. Frisby sees rats marching.
_____

Event 6: _____
_____

Event 7: _____
_____

Event 8: _____
_____

Event 9: Brutus sends Mrs. Frisby away.
_____

Event 10: _____
_____

Event 11: _____
_____

Event 12: _____
_____

Directions:

Using the timeline provided, sequence the following events from Chapters 1-12. Three events have been done for you.

- Mrs. Frisby helps Jeremy.
- Mrs. Frisby asks the owl for help.
- Timothy Frisby becomes ill.
- Mr. Fitzgibbon prepares to plow.
- Mr. Ages prescribes medicine.
- Mrs. Frisby goes to rats' rosebush.
- Mrs. Frisby wonders about the Plan.
- Mrs. Frisby sees rats marching.
- Mrs. Frisby meets Justin.
- Owl learns Mrs. Frisby's identity.
- Brutus sends Mrs. Frisby away.
- Mrs. Frisby is introduced to Nicodemus.

"A Powder for Dragon"

Student Directives

1. Tell about Isabella's encounter with Justin.

2. Detail Nicodemus' talk with Mrs. Frisby.

3. Briefly describe Arthur.

4. Tell how the rats had handled Dragon in the past.

5. Discuss the danger involved with Mrs. Frisby's suggestion to help.

Vocabulary

scrutiny	close observation
recounted	related or told in detail
subsiding	becoming quieter or less

Summary

As Isabella left the others to discuss Mrs. Frisby's problem, she dropped her papers and was obviously delighted that Justin helped her pick them up. Mrs. Frisby retold the events that led her to the rats, including the owl's advice to move her cinder block. Nicodemus, understanding that the owl meant to move the cinder block a few feet so that it would lie behind the stone, drew a sketch of the owl's suggestion so she could understand better. The owl could see from the air that when plowing around a big rock, farmers usually plow close to each side but leave a patch of unplowed land. The stranger, a rat named Arthur, was the chief engineer for the rats. He confirmed that the plan was feasible. The biggest concern was Dragon. Mrs. Frisby feared that the plan would not work, until Justin explained that the rats would slip a sleeping powder, ground by Mr. Ages, into Dragon's food to make him drowsy for about eight hours. To complicate matters, Mr. Ages was the only animal small and quick enough to slip the powder into Dragon's bowl, but his leg was broken. Realizing that she was the only other one small enough to do the job, Mrs. Frisby volunteered. After a brief protest from Justin, the plan was agreed upon. Nicodemus, however, warned Mrs. Frisby that not only had Mr. Ages broken his leg fleeing Dragon, but Mr. Frisby had also died doing the same thing.

"The Marketplace"

Student Directives

1. Briefly tell Mrs. Frisby's reaction to the news of her husband's death.

2. Tell why the rats hadn't discussed Jonathan's death earlier with Mrs. Frisby.

3. Briefly describe Nicodemus' office.

4. Tell Nicodemus' story about NIMH.

Vocabulary

contritely   showing sorrow for having done wrong

commercial   serving purposes of commerce (buying and selling)

converged   came together at one point

flailed   moved about wildly

Summary

Upon hearing the sad circumstances of her late husband's death, Mrs. Frisby buried her head in her arms. The rats had decided not to discuss her husband's death earlier because it would have served no purpose. When Justin and Mr. Ages left to get the sleeping powder, Nicodemus invited Mrs. Frisby into his office to discuss the background of NIMH and her husband's involvement with it. The office was furnished with carpeting, recessed lighting, upholstered furniture, books, and a radio. The story of NIMH, Nicodemus explained, began in a marketplace at the edge of a big city. Although Nicodemus and his family had lived in an underground pipe, they had loved the marketplace with its food and places to play. Nicodemus usually had gone to the market with his older brother and a friend named Jenner, an unusually quick and intelligent rat. One night when Jenner and Nicodemus went to the market alone, they were immediately attracted to a conspicuously large supply of food. Although both rats had noticed a white truck with the letters NIMH printed on it, they didn't find the truck's presence uncommon. As the two rats reached for the food, they were trapped.

Cause and Effect

Name _____

Directions: On the left is a list of causes. On the right is a list of effects. Match the
correct effect with its cause by placing the correct letter in the blank.

A **Cause** produces a result	An **Effect** results from a cause
1. In order to get Timothy the medicine he needed, ____	A. he respected her late husband.
2. Because Jeremy was tangled to the fence with silver string, ____	B. they could help Mrs. Frisby move.
3. When she learned that Mr. Fitzgibbon would begin plowing in five days, ____	C. Mrs. Frisby knew that she needed to move right away.
4. So that she could ask advice from the wise owl, ____	D. Mrs. Frisby went to see Mr. Ages.
5. The owl told Mrs. Frisby to go to the rats because ____	E. Mrs. Frisby decided not to explore the rats' home.
6. Nicodemus was willing to help Mrs. Frisby because ____	F. Mr. Ages was limping from a broken leg.
7. Because she didn't want to upset Nicodemus, ____	G. Mrs. Frisby helped him to get free.
8. Since the rats were too large for the hole in Mrs. Fitzgibbon's kitchen, ____	H. Nicodemus took her to his office and told her the whole story.
9. As a result of his injury from Dragon, ____	I. Mrs. Frisby volunteered to put the powder into Dragon's dish.
10. Since Mrs. Frisby was curious about what had happened at NIMH, ____	J. Jeremy flew Mrs. Frisby to the owl's home deep in the woods.

"In the Cage"

1. Briefly discuss Nicodemus' reaction to getting caught.

2. Tell about the rats' trip to NIMH.

3. Review Dr. Schultz's plan for the rats.

inextricably   in a way that cannot be untied or disentangled

futile   useless

cowered   moved back in fear

At first Nicodemus had no idea why he and the other rats had been captured and carried off in the white truck. Dazed and terrified, Nicodemus did not know where he was being taken. He was also surprised to learn that Jenner, too, had been captured. As the white truck pulled up to a modern building where a laboratory was located, three men joined the others. One of the men was Dr. Schultz, who, Nicodemus would later discover, headed the project at NIMH. The captured rats were placed in individual cages, where they spent a restless first night. Early the next morning, Dr. Schultz returned with two young people also in white coats, George and Julie. As the three people entered the room containing the rats' cages, Dr. Schultz outlined his plan for the rats. He explained that the rats would be divided into three groups with about twenty rats in each group. All the rats' cages would be coded, with each rat being tagged with his own code. All the rats would receive the same diet. At the end of the tagging, injections were to begin. Nicodemus was tagged A-10, and he received injections twice a week. He had no idea what was injected or why. Later, he would discover that for twenty rats, the injections would change their whole lives.

TEST

Mrs. Frisby
and the
Rats of NIMH

Chapters 11-15, Page 1
Name _____

Multiple Choice

Directions:

Circle the letter of the

correct answer.

1. After groping her way through the dark tunnel, Mrs. Frisby was surprised...
   A. that so many rats came to greet her.
   B. by the recessed lights and carpeted floor.
   C. by the electric lights because she had not known anything about electricity.

2. Justin decided to use the grain elevator to make their descent to a lower level because...
   A. Mrs. Frisby was a lady.
   B. it was convenient.
   C. Mr. Ages was limping badly.

3. While waiting in the library, Mrs. Frisby decided against exploring the rats' colony because...
   A. she was worried about getting lost.
   B. she wanted to look at the library books.
   C. Nicodemus had explicitly said to wait in the library.

4. Nicodemus was the rat who was...
   A. the leader of the colony.
   B. the chief engineer of the rats.
   C. the rat of whom Isabella was fond.

5. When Mrs. Frisby had finished telling Nicodemus her story, he...
   A. said that there were many problems with moving the cinder block.
   B. began to draw a sketch of the garden, the rocks, and the cinder block.
   C. said the owl probably didn't understand about plowing.

6. Mrs. Frisby learned that Jonathan Frisby had died when he was...
   A. caught by the men in the white NIMH truck.
   B. slipping powder into Dragon's food.
   C. helping the rats move some electric cable.

7. Nicodemus spent his early years...

    A. in the marketplace at the edge of a big city.

    B. in a cage at NIMH's laboratory.

    C. at the rats' colony near the rosebush.

8. Nicodemus had particularly admired Jenner because he...

    A. was a great athlete.

    B. enjoyed the same activities as Nicodemus did.

    C. was quick and intelligent.

9. Dr. Schultz was...

    A. one of the men who had caught the rats and put them in the white truck.

    B. a famous scientist.

    C. the leader of the laboratory at NIMH.

10. The group of rats who received no injections at all were...

    A. group A.

    B. group B.

    C. group C.

Vocabulary

Directions:

Fill in the blank with the correct word.

detect	irrelevantly	converged
hostile	scrutiny	futile
explicit	recounted	cowered
	contritely	

1. _____ close observation

2. _____ useless

3. _____ showing sorrow for having done wrong

Name _____

4. _____ to discover the presence of

5. _____ plain or clear in language; definite

6. _____ moved back in fear

7. _____ related or told in detail

8. _____ unfriendly, like an enemy; warlike

9. _____ came together at one point

10. _____ in a manner not relating to the subject

Essay Questions

Directions:

Answer in complete

sentences.

1. When the rats had a long project to accomplish, they needed to guard against an attack from Dragon. How did they accomplish this? What kind of animal was needed to do the job?

_____

_____

_____

_____

2. Why did the rats respect Jonathan Frisby so much?

_____

_____

_____

_____

3. Explain how Dr. Schultz grouped the sixty-three rats that were caged at NIMH. What happened to groups A and B? What was different about group C?

_____

_____

_____

_____

"The Maze"

1. Discuss Dr. Schultz's purpose for conducting the experiment.

2. Describe Nicodemus' experiences with the maze.

3. Briefly tell about Justin's escape.

4. Relate Julie's reaction to Justin's escape.

5. Discuss what Justin learned from Dr. Schultz's conversation with his assistants.

Vocabulary

emerged	came forth into view
illusion	something that deceives by producing a false impression
underestimating	placing at too low a value

Summary

During the days that followed, the rats realized that they were part of an experiment. Dr. Schultz was a neurologist who wanted to learn whether certain injections could help the rats learn more and faster. Dr. Schultz and the two graduate students in biology, George and Julie, expected group A would learn fastest of all. When Nicodemus first began his training, he thought that he was being set free, but when he tried to reach the outdoors, he was met by an electric shock. Nicodemus was placed in a maze, a device to test memory and intelligence, and the trick was to run through it as quickly as possible. In other tests, the rats had to learn shape recognition in order to escape electric shock. One of the rats, named Justin, whose cage was next to Nicodemus, decided he would try to escape when his cage was open for injections. The next morning, when Justin made his leap, Julie merely pushed a button on the wall. Dr. Schultz and his assistants had expected an escape, and they were delighted that the rats were so intelligent. While out of his cage, Justin discovered that there were mice being held in cages as well and that soon they would be given injections of steroids in addition to their regular injections.

"A Lesson in Reading"

1. Briefly discuss what Justin learned during his brief escape.

2. Relate what was happening to group A and group B mice.

3. Briefly describe how the rats learned to read.

4. Tell how Dr. Schultz's caution was his undoing.

5. Discuss how reading helped Justin get out of his cage.

Vocabulary

submitted	yielded in surrender
incurring	receiving as a consequence of some action
ritual	a series of acts done in the same way every time

Summary

Justin's escape was brief. He was put back in his cage, but he did learn that he could jump from his cage without getting hurt or making the scientists angry. During the months to follow, the group A rats were learning more and more and becoming more intelligent than the other rats. Because group A was given a new series of injections, they were outliving all the other rats as well. Group B was given a different formula of the same injections, but they didn't live as long as group A. Dr. Schultz wanted all research kept top secret since he was planning to publish the results in a scientific journal. Reading was the most important phase of the rats' training. The rats were learning to read through a series of pictures, shapes, and sounds. Once Nicodemus understood the idea, he could hardly wait for the next lessons. He was soon reading far more than Dr. Schultz had anticipated. Not wanting to risk failure, Dr. Schultz was too cautious about testing the rats, and they began plotting their eventual escape. Justin learned that by reading the instructions on his cage door, he could get out and explore, investigating different ways to escape.

The Lab at NIMH

Name _____

When scientists choose animals for their research, they select small mammals that will react in a manner similar to human beings. From your reading of the novel, you can understand why rats and mice are often used in scientific experimentation.

In order to produce accurate test results, scientists must create a controlled environment and record their results in an organized way. After Dr. Schultz and his aides had captured Justin, Jenner, and the others, they intended to follow certain scientific testing procedures. First, they must control all variables in the testing. Second, they must devise DNA and steroid treatments for certain groups. Third, they must establish a control group of rats which would not receive any DNA or steroid treatments. And fourth, once they had established and followed their procedures, they must then compare the results, interpret their findings, and draw conclusions from the testing.

You know from your reading that the injections did have marked results. But you don't know what Dr. Schultz finally did with the information that he gained from his experiments.

Let's be a bit more precise about how scientists collect information. Using the following chart, tet's organize the data that you have been presented about the experiment.

The Lab at NIMH

Name _____

Directions:	Here is a chart that Dr. Schultz, Julie, and George might have used to compare the lab results among the various groups of rats and mice they tested at NIMH. Fill in the chart, using the following pages from the novel to get your information: page 108; pages 111-115; page 118; and page 121.

NIMH Testing of DNA and Steroids

•Lab Input•

	Group A-Rats	Group B-Rats	Group C-Rats	Group G-Mice
Number in Group				8 mice
Food Type				scientific pellets
Living Conditions				cages
Testing Methods				mazes/shape recognition
DNA Injections				strong dosage
Steroid Injections				strong dosage
Injection Frequency				twice a week

•Lab Outcome•

	Group A-Rats	Group B-Rats	Group C-Rats	Group G-Mice
Learning Speed				300% ahead of group C
Stimulus Reactions				300% ahead of group C
Longevity				more than double lifespan

Note: In real-life testing, scientists would have completely determined the DNA results before introducing steroids into the testing. Also, scientific measurements of dosages would have been recorded. In the novel, steroids are presented as completely beneficial, but in real life, prolonged use of steroids can produce serious medical complications.

"The Air Ducts"

Student Directives

1. Discuss Justin's escape plan, including the equipment needed.

2. Discuss what information the rats learned from exploring.

3. Review Jonathan's request to Nicodemus.

4. Discuss Jenner's concerns about what the rats would do after escaping.

5. Discuss the mice's problem with the escape.

Vocabulary

astute	shrewd; cunning
plaintive	mournful; sorrowful
consternation	bewilderment; alarm
strode	walked with long steps

Summary

Justin saw the air ducts and realized that he had to find and explore the main air shaft. Jenner, astutely realizing that they could easily get lost in the ducts, used a large spool of thread and a screwdriver to keep from getting lost in the dark shafts. Justin's hunch to follow the fresher, harder-blowing air proved correct, and after finding the main motor, he discovered the shaft that led to the open sky. Across the opening was, as Jenner predicted, a wire screen. The rats met that night to plan their escape the following evening. As the meeting ended, the small voice of a mouse asked Nicodemus to set the mice free as well. This was the voice of Jonathan. Nicodemus agreed to do so. On the night before their escape, Jenner was worried about the rats' adjustment to life on the outside. They could never go back to living the life they had known before NIMH. The next night, the mice were to escape along with the rats to freedom. However, the force of the main motor was too much for the tiny creatures and six were blown away—their fate never to be known. The remaining two mice were able to help the rats by squeezing under the screen and loosening it with the screwdriver. At last, the rats and two mice were free!

"The Boniface Estate"

1. Discuss the journey of the rats and the two mice after their escape.

2. Describe the reaction of other rats to the superior NIMH rats.

3. Describe where the rats, Jonathan, and Mr. Ages spent their first winter.

4. Tell about the one thing the rats had to watch out for.

Vocabulary

discontent	dissatisfaction
cursory	hasty; superficial

Summary

The rats, Jonathan, and Mr. Ages began a journey that lasted almost two years. Parts of the journey were joyful, and parts were filled with trouble and danger. Adjusting to life on the outside was difficult. The NIMH rats and mice found that other rats looked on them strangely. They seemed to sense that the NIMH rats were different. One day during their travels, they came upon a large, deserted-looking estate surrounded by an expensive fence. The house appeared empty, so they found a window with a cracked pane and climbed in. Learning that this was a rich person's mansion and that the newly married owners were on an extended honeymoon, the rats and mice settled into the luxurious home. The house was well stocked with food, the surroundings were beautiful, and the library was filled with books. The only interruption during their stay at the Boniface Estate was the caretaker, so the rats posted a watch and made sure the house was always kept in a presentable condition.

"The Main Hall"

Student Directives

1. Discuss what Mrs. Frisby decided to tell her children.

2. Review Mrs. Frisby's impressions of the main hall.

3. Tell what "the Plan" was and how the rats were preparing for it.

Vocabulary

skeptical	having doubt
confer	consult together; compare opinions
portal	door, gate, or entrance

Summary

Mrs. Frisby had been so engrossed in Nicodemus' story about the NIMH rats and mice that she had forgotten to feed her children their lunch. She didn't want the children to worry about the danger of moving the cinder block, so she decided to say nothing about their father's association with NIMH or about her part in helping to drug Dragon. Returning to the rats' home that night, Mrs. Frisby was shown the main hall, the largest room she had ever seen. The hall was a flurry of activity with many rats working everywhere under brightly lit electric lights. Some rats worked with tools, but most hauled large sacks. Explaining that all the activity was related to the Plan, Justin showed Mrs. Frisby their most important invention—a plow made to be pulled by rats. In another room, Mrs. Frisby saw stockpiles of corn, barley, and soy beans, plus many boxes of seeds. Justin explained that the rats' Plan was to grow their own food—to live without stealing.

Mrs. Frisby
and the
Rats of NIMH

About the Characters, Part 2

Name_____

Directions: Below is a Character Chart to help you organize the characters from the novel. Fill in whatever information is missing—either the character's name or a character summary. Use this list of characters for the Character Chart.

Dr. Schultz	Nicodemus	Jenner	Toy Tinker
Julie	Isabella	Paul	Justin
George	Arthur	Billy	Mrs. Fitzgibbon

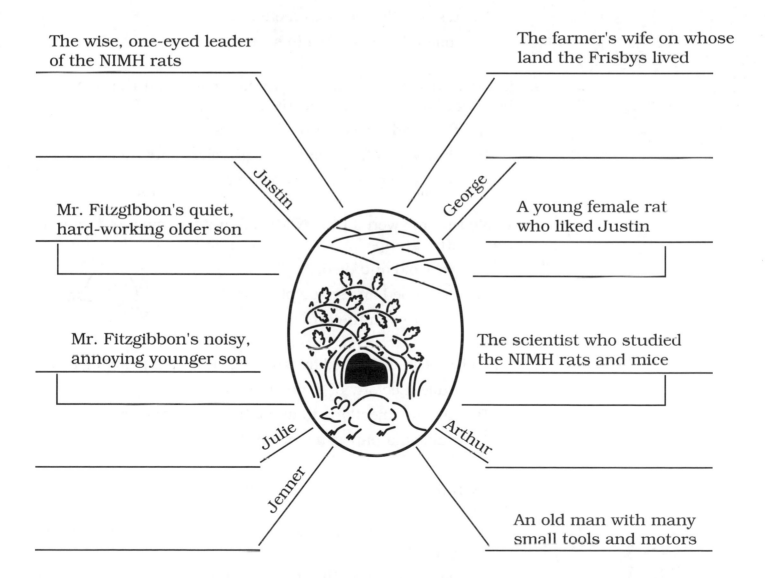

The wise, one-eyed leader of the NIMH rats

The farmer's wife on whose land the Frisbys lived

Justin

George

Mr. Fitzgibbon's quiet, hard-working older son

A young female rat who liked Justin

Mr. Fitzgibbon's noisy, annoying younger son

The scientist who studied the NIMH rats and mice

Julie

Arthur

Jenner

An old man with many small tools and motors

Multiple Choice

Directions:

Circle the letter of the

correct answer.

1. In the experiment at NIMH, group A was the most fortunate group because they...

    A. received better food.

    B. were allowed to get out of their cages.

    C. were given injections to make them smarter.

2. The maze used by the scientists was a device to:

    A. make rats run faster.

    B. test intelligence and memory.

    C. make the rats learn to suffer pain.

3. If Justin had been caught escaping, he felt that the scientists wouldn't hurt him because...

    A. they had grown fond of the rats.

    B. they were afraid that the rats might bite them.

    C. the rats were too valuable to them.

4. While the rats were in the NIMH laboratory, most of them in the Control group C...

    A. grew old and died.

    B. developed an escape plan.

    C. tried to join the rats in group A.

5. When Dr. Schultz finished his experiment, he was planning to...

    A. build a colony of super-intelligent rats.

    B. use his injections to make humans smarter.

    C. publish a paper in a scientific journal.

6. Dr. Schultz's mistake in dealing with the rats' reading ability was that he...

    A. was afraid to test the rats to see how much they had learned.

    B. gave injections that were too powerful.

    C. didn't put fool proof locks on the rats' cages.

7. When the rats escaped their cages at night, they needed to find...

    A. an open window.

    B. the main air shaft of the air-conditioning unit.

    C. the key to the door.

8. Exploring the air ducts at night was difficult because...

    A. they couldn't find any string.

    B. it was completely dark.

    C. they kept running into trap doors.

9. On the night before their planned escape, Jenner was worried that...

    A. the mice would get in the rats' way.

    B. they wouldn't have enough time to escape.

    C. they wouldn't be able to fit in with rats in the outside world.

10. After the rats escaped, their first important piece of luck was...

    A. finding other rats to join them.

    B. discovering a large, deserted estate.

    C. finding discarded food in garbage cans.

Vocabulary

Directions:

Fill in the blank with the correct word.

illusion	astute	cursory
submitted	plaintive	skeptical
ritual	strode	portal
	discontent	

1. _____   hasty; superficial

2. _____   mournful

3. _____   something that deceives by producing a false impression

TEST

Mrs. Frisby
and the
Rats of NIMH

Chapters 16-20, Page 3

Name _____

4. _____ dissatisfaction

5. _____ door, gate, or entrance

6. _____ a series of acts done in the same way
   _____ every time

7. _____ having doubt

8. _____ shrewd; cunning

9. _____ walked with long steps

10. _____ yielded in surrender

Essay Questions

Directions:

Answer in complete

sentences.

1. Explain why finding the air ducts was so important to the rats'
   escape plan.

   _____

   _____

   _____

2. Explain how the spool of thread and the screwdriver were
   necessary for the rats' escape.

   _____

   _____

   _____

3. On the night before their escape, Jenner confided to
   Nicodemus that he was worried about how the NIMH rats
   would get along on the outside if their plan was successful.
   What was the main reason for his concern?

   _____

   _____

   _____

"The Toy Tinker"

Student Directives

1. Tell what the rats needed after leaving the Boniface Estate.

2. Discuss how the rats' reading affected their decision-making.

3. Review why the rats wanted their own type of civilization.

4. Relate why the rats chose land near the Thorn Mountains National Forest as their home.

5. Briefly describe the rats' encounter with the Toy Tinker.

Vocabulary

scavengers	those who feed on discarded food
civilization	an advanced state of human society in which a high level of art, science, religion, and government has been reached
heirs	othose who inherit the property of a deceased person

Summary

The rats needed to find a permanent place to live after their stay at Boniface Estate. They read during the winter on a great many subjects, but what Nicodemus had liked best was history. Nicodemus was inspired by his reading to develop a civilization designed for the super-intelligent rats. From his reading Nicodemus also learned that rats had long been despised because they supposedly carried disease, stole food, and bit children. He learned that millions of years ago rats seemed more advanced than other animals, but after a while they stopped progressing, perhaps because their lives were too easy. The rats discussed how their civilization should develop. They knew they wanted a civilization different from that of humans. For example, the rats wanted an underground civilization, preferably in a cave near farmland. After much studying, they decided to live at the edge of the Thorn Mountains National Forest. One day before finding their present cave, the rats came across the body of the Toy Tinker, who had died, apparently while attempting to dig his truck out of a ditch. They buried the elderly tinker and decided to put his truck to use.

"Thorn Valley"

Student Directives

1. Briefly discuss what the rats discovered in the Toy Tinker's truck.

2. Relate why the rats became discontented in their comfortable colony on the Fitzgibbon farm.

3. Tell why the rats decided to move to Thorn Valley.

4. Briefly describe Jenner's outlook on life.

5. Describe the rats' preparation for the Plan.

Vocabulary

reluctant	unwilling; hesitant
precautions	measures taken beforehand to secure good results
cynical	distrusting the motives of others
pessimist	one who looks on the gloomy side of things

Summary

The rats discovered more than toys in the Tinker's truck. There were utensils, simple furniture, and a small refrigerator with canned food. But the real finds were electric motors of all sizes and tiny tools for repairing the toys. With these treasures, the rats were able to plug into Mr. Fitzgibbon's underground power cable and water pipe to provide them with all the electricity and water they would need. After completing the initial activities of developing the colony, the rats were overcome by a lingering discontent. Feeling that they had joined the "People Race," the rats called a series of meetings to decide their future—a future with purpose. As he went about trying to find the perfect place to relocate, Nicodemus met some chipmunks in his travels who thought he should seek the owl's advice. The owl suggested moving to Thorn Valley, which lay deep in the forest. Nicodemus explored the valley and wanted to move. Jenner, on the other hand, was pessimistic about moving away from the comfortable life they had created at Mr. Fitzgibbon's farm. He felt it was only right to steal from man since man had no problem taking things from other animals. Most of the rats, however, wanted to try living independently of the farm, and so the Plan was adopted. The rats began stockpiling food and seeds and making tools so they could move to Thorn Valley in June.

Outlining

Name _____

Use after Chapter 22.

Outlining is an essential skill for organizing your thoughts and learning new material. Below is an article written about the Plan of the NIMH rats. Read the article and consult the Topics List to complete the outline. Some topics have been filled in for you.

Remember that outlines are divided into main topics, sub-topics, and supporting information. Use the article, "The Plan," as a model for outlining.

The Plan

Use the accompanying students' sheets to complete the outlining.

Mrs. Frisby was very impressed with the NIMH rats during her first meeting with them. The rats' home, equipped with electricity, was clean and attractive. After greeting her warmly, both Justin and Nicodemus were willing to do all they could to help with Moving Day. Like the owl, Justin and Nicodemus greatly respected Jonathan Frisby. Mrs. Frisby saw much that aroused her curiosity in the rats' home. Of all the intriguing ideas she encountered during her visit, however, the most interesting was "the Plan."

After Mrs. Frisby had earned the rats' confidence, Justin carefully explained the Plan. Taking her down a long, winding tunnel, Justin led Mrs. Frisby to the main hall. The size, the noise, and the activity left Mrs. Frisby dizzy with amazement. The large, brightly lit room was filled with working rats—some worked on machines, like saws or grindstones, but most were hauling.

The size of the main hall, almost 20 feet square, was staggering to a small animal like Mrs. Frisby. Justin explained that the room was a natural cave, occupied in former centuries by bears, wolves, foxes, and ground hogs. Because of its size, the cave was the rats' chief workshop.

One especially busy group of rats was working on a device which looked like a boat but was actually a plow for rats. Designed by Nicodemus, the plow was small and light enough to be pulled by eight rats. With a hard day's work, the rats could plow a small patch of earth to grow their own food. After successfully constructing a pilot model, the rats were busy constructing three more plows.

Outlining

Name_____

Leading Mrs. Frisby to the back of the cave, Justin showed her a large wooden bin, housing a mountain of oats. Other bins contained similar supplies of barley, corn, and soy beans. Justin explained that the rats had been stockpiling for a long time and that they now had a two-year grain supply to feed one hundred and eight rats, plus enough to plant two crops. In the last bin, the rats had stored seeds for tomatoes, beets, carrots, and melons. After learning that the rats' Plan was to build their own rat civilization and live their lives without stealing, Mrs. Frisby was even more impressed with them.

Mrs. Frisby learned later, during a long conversation with Nicodemus, about the location of the rats' new home. Nicodemus had heard about Thorn Valley from the owl, who knew every tree and trail in the forest. Once Nicodemus viewed the natural splendor of Thorn Valley, nestled safely in the deep woods, he realized that it was the perfect place to build a rat civilization.

Directions: An incomplete outline for "The Plan" is given in the left column. Choose from the right column to complete the outline. Parts of the outline have been properly placed for you.

The Plan	Topics List
I. The Rats' Main Hall	**I.** The Rats' Main Hall
A. Description	used in the past
1. _____	filled with working rats
2. _____	almost 20 feet square
B. Size—_____	large, bright room
C. History	natural cave
1. _____	
2. _____	

Outlining

Name _____

The Plan (con't)

II. The Rats' Plow

  A. Design

    1. _____

    2. _____

    3. _____

  B. Usefulness

    1. _____

    2. _____

III. Storage Bins

  A. Grains

    1. Types

      a. _____

      b. _____

      c. _____

    2. Quantities

      a. _____

      b. _____

  B. Fruit and Vegetable Seeds

IV. Plan's Purpose

  A. _____

  B. _____

V. Thorn Valley

  A. _____

  B. _____

  C. _____

Topics List

II. The Rats' Plow

  plow earth

  small and light

  grow own food

  by Nicodemus

  pulled by 8 rats

III. Storage Bins

  2-year supply

  soy beans

  barley

  feed 108 rats

  corn

IV. Plan's Purpose

  Live without stealing

  Build rat civilization

V. Thorn Valley

  Advice from owl

  Beautiful, safe spot

  Location of new home

"Captured"

Student Directives

1. Discuss Mrs. Frisby's questions about her husband and NIMH.

2. Tell about the secret Jonathan kept from Mrs. Frisby.

3. Tell what Mrs. Frisby learned about Jenner.

3. Relate how Mrs. Frisby slipped Dragon the powder and was captured.

Vocabulary

solitude	the state of living or being alone
denounced	condemned openly
admonished	scolded in a good-natured way

Summary

Mr. Ages alerted Mrs. Frisby and the rats, so they could get their evening maneuvers organized. Mrs. Frisby, though, had a few more questions about her husband and NIMH. She learned that after a time Jonathan and Mr. Ages left the rat colony to live like mice again. Mr. Ages sought solitude, but Jonathan sought the company of other mice. Once married, he was never able to reveal the extent of his differences from other mice—that he would live longer and stay younger. Mrs. Frisby was also curious about Jenner, who was angered not only by the rats' determination to move but also by their decision to destroy all their machines so they wouldn't be tempted to return to the Fitzgibbon farm when times got tough. She learned that Jenner stomped out of the meeting with six followers, leaving the colony forever. After her questions had been answered, the time that Mrs. Frisby had dreaded arrived. Justin and Mr. Ages walked with her to the farmhouse, giving directions as they went. After a bit of maneuvering, Mrs. Frisby found the hole to the Fitzgibbons' kitchen. She entered only to find that Dragon's bowl was farther from the cabinet than usual. She raced across the room and poured the powder into Dragon's bowl. Suddenly the lights went dim, and Mrs. Frisby was trapped in a curved metal cage—a colander— which had been placed over her by the Fitzgibbons' son, Billy.

"Seven Dead Rats"

1. Discuss Billy's plans for Mrs. Frisby.

2. Review what Mrs. Frisby learned about the incident at Henderson's hardware store.

3. Review why the rats would be in danger from the Public Health Service.

4. Discuss why Mr. Fitzgibbon had already decided to destroy the rat colony.

Vocabulary

retreated	drew back for shelter or seclusion
resume	to continue after an interruption
incinerated	burned or reduced to ashes

Summary

Billy Fitzgibbon placed Mrs. Frisby in a bird cage which had formerly been occupied by his pet canary. Mrs. Frisby was sick with worry because Billy was planning to keep her for several days. Her only consolation was that Dragon had greedily eaten his dinner—powder and all. During their dinner, the Fitzgibbons discussed an incident involving a group of rats which had accidentally electrocuted themselves at Henderson's hardware store. When the article about the rats appeared in the newspaper, the Public Health Service from the federal government became involved. They were planning to exterminate all the rats in the area with cyanide gas. Mr. Fitzgibbon assumed that the Public Health Service would want to bulldoze the rosebush on his farm to get rid of his rats. Even if the government hadn't gotten involved, Mr. Fitzgibbon was planning to exterminate the rats himself because they had been stealing too much food and too many seeds. Mrs. Frisby now had two urgent reasons for wanting to escape—caring for her children and warning Nicodemus of the impending danger.

Newspaper Writing

Name _____

In Chapter 24 of *Mrs. Frisby and the Rats of NIMH*, Mrs. Frisby is caged in the Fitzgibbons' kitchen. While the Fitzgibbons were eating dinner, Mrs. Frisby heard Mr. Fitzgibbon talking about an odd occurrence that had taken place at Henderson's hardware store.

According to Mr. Fitzgibbon, six or seven rats had invaded the store and were trying to move some of the electric motors. After gnawing at the insulation, the rats had gotten electrocuted.

With all the publicity about the rats, the Public Health Service had gotten involved and was planning to exterminate all the area rats. Mr. Fitzgibbon said that a "Doctor somebody" was in charge of the operation. When she heard the news, Mrs. Frisby knew that she had to escape soon to warn her friends, the rats.

Directions:

Pretend that you are a star reporter for the Daily Gazette. Write a newspaper article, giving all the important facts of the rats' invasion at Henderson's hardware store. Also include the plans of the Public Health Service.

Be sure to answer all of the reporter questions: Who? What? When? Where? Why? and How? Use pages 190-193 of the novel to help you with the background. When information is not given, use your imagination to fill in the details that a reporter might from interviewing people. You might also include some direct quotes to make your article more authentic.

Mechanized Rats Invade Hardware Store

By _____

"Escape"

Student Directives

1. Relate how Justin saved Mrs. Frisby.

2. Discuss Justin's reaction to Mrs. Frisby's news.

3. Briefly review the rats' efforts to move the Frisby home.

Vocabulary

defective   faulty; imperfect

impasse   a situation that prevents progress

defiant   characterized by bold opposition

commenced   began; started

Summary

After the Fitzgibbons had put out the cat and gone to bed, Mrs. Frisby tried to escape, but she was unsuccessful. She heard a small scuffling noise; Justin had returned. He scurried up a window curtain and leaped onto the cage. Justin feared that the Fitzgibbons would become suspicious if he were to open the heavy door to the cage, so he tampered with the flimsy little rings to make them look defective and then set Mrs. Frisby free. As they hurried to the cinder block, Mrs. Frisby told about the conversation she had heard concerning the exterminators and the cyanide gas. Justin looked at Mrs. Frisby admiringly and said he knew from the first that she would bring good luck. There was a more immediate problem, though. Mrs. Frisby's neighbor, the shrew, was standing defiantly in front of the cinder block and causing a problem for the rats. Mrs. Frisby arrived and assured the shrew that the rats had permission to move her home. The rats could now efficiently and swiftly move Mrs. Frisby's cinder block to safety. It was a well-organized undertaking which included heavy-duty moving equipment. The rats also dug tunnels and holes which would have taken Mrs. Frisby all day to do.

Explaining Information

Name_____

Imagine that you are in Mrs. Frisby's situation. You are trapped in a cage and can't escape, yet you need to warn your friends, the rats, about the impending danger. The only difference between you and Mrs. Frisby is that you have the ability to write and have a way to send your letter. If you could send a letter to warn your friends, how would you write it? Remember that you can send only one letter, and it must contain all the vital information, or your friends will surely die. In your letter, be sure to answer all the reporter questions—Who? What? When? Where? Why? How?

Dear Nicodemus,

I am writing to warn you about _____

_____

_____

_____

_____

_____

_____

_____

_____

_____

_____

_____

_____

_____

_____

TEST

Mrs. Frisby
and the
Rats of NIMH

Chapters 21-25, Page 1

Name _____

Multiple Choice

Directions:

Circle the letter of the

correct answer.

1. It seemed to the rats that the main reason they were so hated was that they...

    A. were so ugly.

    B. always lived by stealing.

    C. bit human children.

2. When it came time to leave the Boniface Estate, the rats were not sorry to move out because...

    A. it was never natural or comfortable for them.

    B. there was not enough food for them.

    C. they were always worried that the caretaker would find them.

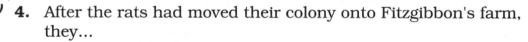

3. When the rats uncovered the contents of the Toy Tinker's truck, what they liked most were...

    A. the electric motors.

    B. the toys.

    C. the miniature tools.

4. After the rats had moved their colony onto Fitzgibbon's farm, they...

    A. were very happy.

    B. were affected with discontent.

    C. wanted to move back to the Boniface Estate.

5. Nicodemus didn't want to stay at Fitzgibbon's farm because...

    A. he thought Thorn Valley was more beautiful.

    B. he wanted more room.

    C. everything the rats had at Fitzgibbon's farm was stolen.

6. Jonathan never told Mrs. Frisby about his experiences at NIMH because...

    A. the rats asked him to keep it a secret.

    B. he was a liar.

    C. he thought the news would distress her.

TEST

Mrs. Frisby
and the
Rats of NIMH

Chapters 21-25, Page 2

Name _____

7. Jenner denounced the other rats as "idiots and dreamers" because...

    A. he didn't like working as hard as the other rats did.

    B. the rats were planning to destroy all their machines.

    C. he wasn't as smart as the other rats.

8. The rats that invaded Henderson's hardware store were killed by...

    A. eating rat poison.

    B. breathing cyanide gas.

    C. being electrocuted.

9. When Mr. Fitzgibbon found out that the Public Health Service was going to bulldoze his rosebush, he was...

    A. angry that they would destroy his property.

    B. happy because he was planning on exterminating the rats himself.

    C. worried about the harm to his crops.

10. When Justin rescued Mrs. Frisby from the cage, he didn't lift the cage door because...

    A. it was too heavy for him.

    B. he couldn't figure out how the door lock worked.

    C. he didn't want the Fitzgibbons to suspect anything.

Vocabulary

Directions:

Fill in the blank with

the correct word.

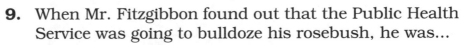

scavengers	cynical	retreated
heirs	pessimist	defective
reluctant	solitude	defiant
	admonished	

1. _____ scolded in a good-natured way

2. _____ faulty; imperfect

3. _____ those who inherit the property of a deceased person

4. _____   distrusting the motives of others

5. _____   unwilling; hesitant

6. _____   characterized by bold opposition

7. _____   those who feed on discarded food

8. _____   the state of living or being alone

9. _____   one who looks on the gloomy side of things

10. _____   drew back for shelter or seclusion

Essay Questions

Directions:

Answer in complete sentences.

1. The rats living on Fitzgibbon's farm decided that they wanted to create their own rat civilization. What does it mean to build a civilization? What luxuries would the rats have to give up in order to make a new life at Thorn Valley?

   _____

   _____

   _____

2. Jenner and Nicodemus differed in their attitudes about the Plan. Explain how each of them felt.

   _____

   _____

   _____

3. While Mrs. Frisby was trapped in a cage in the kitchen, she overheard some alarming news about the rats. What was the danger for the rat colony near the rosebush? Be specific about *who*, *what*, *when*, *where*, *why*, and *how*.

   _____

   _____

   _____

"At the Meeting"

Student Directives

1. Discuss why the rats sent for Mrs. Frisby after her escape.

2. Review their main concern about the seven electrocuted rats.

3. Tell why the rats were concerned about the Public Health Service.

4. Relate the rats' plan to cover their tracks.

5. Discuss why ten rats were needed to form a rear guard.

Vocabulary

presumed	took for granted; supposed
cryptically	in a secretive manner

Summary

   The morning after moving Mrs. Frisby's house, the rats sent for her and brought her into the large assembly room to question her in detail about the conversation she had heard in the Fitzgibbons' kitchen. In particular, they were concerned that the "mechanized" rats reported in the newspaper might be Jenner and his followers. They were also worried that the doctor might be from NIMH. If the NIMH scientists knew that the super-intelligent rats were in the area, they would want the rats captured or killed, since they feared the rats' intelligence. Mrs. Frisby warned them that the Public Health Service planned to bulldoze and exterminate the area by the rosebush. The rats would not have time to destroy their motors, books, and furniture, so they decided to move them into the cave and bury them, sealing off all rooms but one and covering all clues of their colony. In order to make the scene more realistic, they decided to put garbage in the storage room and to leave behind ten rats (Justin and Brutus were among at least fifty who volunteered) as a rear guard. Despite the obvious danger, the rear guard planned to escape through a hidden exit as soon as the exterminators made any noise.

"The Doctor"

Student Directives

1. Tell what Mr. Fitzgibbon did the day after the rats' assembly.

2. Briefly describe Mrs. Frisby's reactions to the extermination activities.

3. Describe the extermination process.

4. Explain the strategy of the rear guard rats.

5. Discuss the heroism of the rat who saved Brutus.

Vocabulary

inexorable	unstoppable; unalterable; inevitable
donned	put on
antidote	a medicine or remedy to counteract the effects of poison

Summary

The day after the rats' assembly, Mr. Fitzgibbon started his tractor in anticipation of the exterminators. At first, Mrs. Frisby thought she couldn't watch the destruction of her friends' home, but she soon decided that it was worse not to watch. When the exterminators in the white truck arrived, they examined the rosebush and agreed that they would need to bulldoze the colony. After struggling to level the rosebush, the men in the white suits unrolled a long, flexible pipe with a plunger apparatus attached to one end. Donning a protective mask, one man prepared to gas the rat hole. Once the gassing began, seven rats of the rear guard ran back and forth in hectic fashion, causing the exterminators to believe that many rats were running from the colony. After a time, an eighth rat emerged from the hole, running and stumbling into the thicket. When the extermination was complete, Mrs. Frisby rushed to the thicket to find that Brutus had been overcome by the gas. As soon as the exterminators left, Mr. Ages was beside him with an antidote. When he recovered, Brutus explained that one of the rats had pulled him to safety and then rushed in to save another rat. Sadly, both rats had perished in the hole.

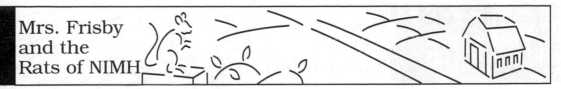

Character Development

Use after
Chapter 27.

Robert C. O'Brien introduces his readers to a vast array of imaginative, well-developed characters in *Mrs. Frisby and the Rats of NIMH*. Two of the most memorable characters in the novel are Nicodemus, the thoughtful, organized leader of the NIMH rats, and Jenner, the critical, rebellious defector.

Although both rats were exposed to the same situations, their reactions, feelings, and philosophies were directly opposed to each other. Jenner, on the one hand, was cynical about life. Lacking Nicodemus' grand vision of a true rat civilization, Jenner was completely satisfied with his easy, comfortable life of stealing. Nicodemus, on the other hand, believed that with conviction, organization, and hard work, there is a better way of life for the rats. Nicodemus was willing to sacrifice his easy life to build a true rat civilization.

Good literature, like *Mrs. Frisby and the Rats of NIMH*, serves not only to entertain and educate us, but also to enrich us spiritually. In analyzing the characters of Jenner and Nicodemus, not only do we learn about their character development, but we are also given examples of how we can strive to conduct our own lives.

The Discovering Literature Series focuses on ten character virtues:

Responsibility	Friendship
Courage	Persistence
Compassion	Hard Work
Loyalty	Self-discipline
Honesty	Faith

The following pages apply many of these virtues to Nicodemus and Jenner. Use examples from the novel to compare the virtues—or lack of virtues—of Nicodemus and Jenner.

Mrs. Frisby and the Rats of NIMH

Character Development, Page 1

Name _____

| Directions: | In the left column are listed character virtues. Give examples from the novel which illustrate these virutes or lack of these virtues for Nicodemus and Jenner. |

	Jenner	**Nicodemus**
Responsibility		
Courage		
Compassion		
Loyalty		
Honesty		

**Mrs. Frisby
and the
Rats of NIMH**

Character Development, Page 2

Name _____

	Jenner	**Nicodemus**
Friendship	_____	_____
	_____	_____
	_____	_____
Persistence	_____	_____
	_____	_____
	_____	_____
Hard Work	_____	_____
	_____	_____
	_____	_____
Self-discipline	_____	_____
	_____	_____
	_____	_____

Which philosophy—Jenner's or Nicodemus'—worked better in the long run? Why?

_____

_____

_____

_____

_____

"Epilogue"

Student Directives

1. Discuss the Fitzgibbons' planting.

2. Review Mrs. Frisby's thoughts about her rat friends.

3. Briefly tell about Mrs. Frisby's discussion with her children after they had moved.

4. Discuss which rat the Frisbys thought had died.

5. Tell how the Frisbys thought they could contact the rats.

Vocabulary

frenzy   violent agitation; wild excitement

harrow   farm implement used to level plowed land

deliberation   careful consideration before a decision

incredulously   in an unbelieving manner

Summary

A few days after the extermination, Mrs. Frisby heard the Fitzgibbons' tractor preparing soil for planting. She had no reason to worry, for the rats had calculated wisely, and her home was safe. She reflected on the whereabout of her friends, the rats, wondering if she would ever see them again. On a warm day in May, Mrs. Frisby and her children left the cinder block to move to their summer home in a winter wheat field. Once the family was situated, Mrs. Frisby told them the story of their father's and the rats' involvement at NIMH. She was surprised that Timothy had already guessed part of the truth. When she reached the end of the story, the children became very emotional. The Frisbys knew that one brave rat had saved Brutus and had reentered the rat hole to save another, and they feared that the brave rat had been Justin. The Frisbys settled into their summer home with many unanswered questions about their rat friends. When fall would come, the Frisbys hoped to see Jeremy the crow, who might be able to help them visit their friends at Thorn Valley.

Plot Development

Authors must plan for three major elements—characters, setting, and plot—when creating a story. Of the three narrative elements, plot is usually the most difficult to develop.

In every well-developed plot, the central character has a problem, or conflict, to overcome. The central problem can be a conflict between two people, between a character and the society in which she or he lives, between a character and nature, or it could even be a conflict within the main character. Whatever the conflict, the main character works through his or her problem throughout the novel or script. In doing so, the main character encounters a series of minor problems, or difficulties; however, these are all directed toward resolving the major conflict.

The structure of a plot can be compared to climbing a mountain. At the base of the mountain, the reader is introduced to the main characters and to the setting. As the story develops, the reader is presented with a major problem to be overcome. All the while, the reader is steadily climbing the mountain until he or she reaches the peak, where the action reaches a turning point or climax. As soon as the climax has been reached, the action falls rapidly—just as a mountain climber would when rushing down the back side of a mountain. Once the action falls, the reader sees the central character resolve her or his problem.

The Plot Organization Map graphically illustrates how the plot is developed. Using the following Rising Action topics and Falling Action topics, complete the Plot Organization Map. Plot the events sequentially and then fill in the characters, setting, problem, and resolution.

Duplicate the Plot Organization Map on oversize paper for ease of student use.

Rising Action

•Mrs. Frisby meets owl.

•Rats move cinder block.

•Mrs. Frisby needs to move.

•Mrs. Frisby learns of the Plan.

•Timothy becomes ill.

•Mrs. Frisby learns of exterminators.

•NIMH rats agree to help.

•Timothy cannot be moved.

•The exterminators come.

•Mrs. Frisby slips powder to Dragon.

Falling Action

•Mrs. Frisby's family moves to summer home.

•All rats, but two, escape to Thorn Valley.

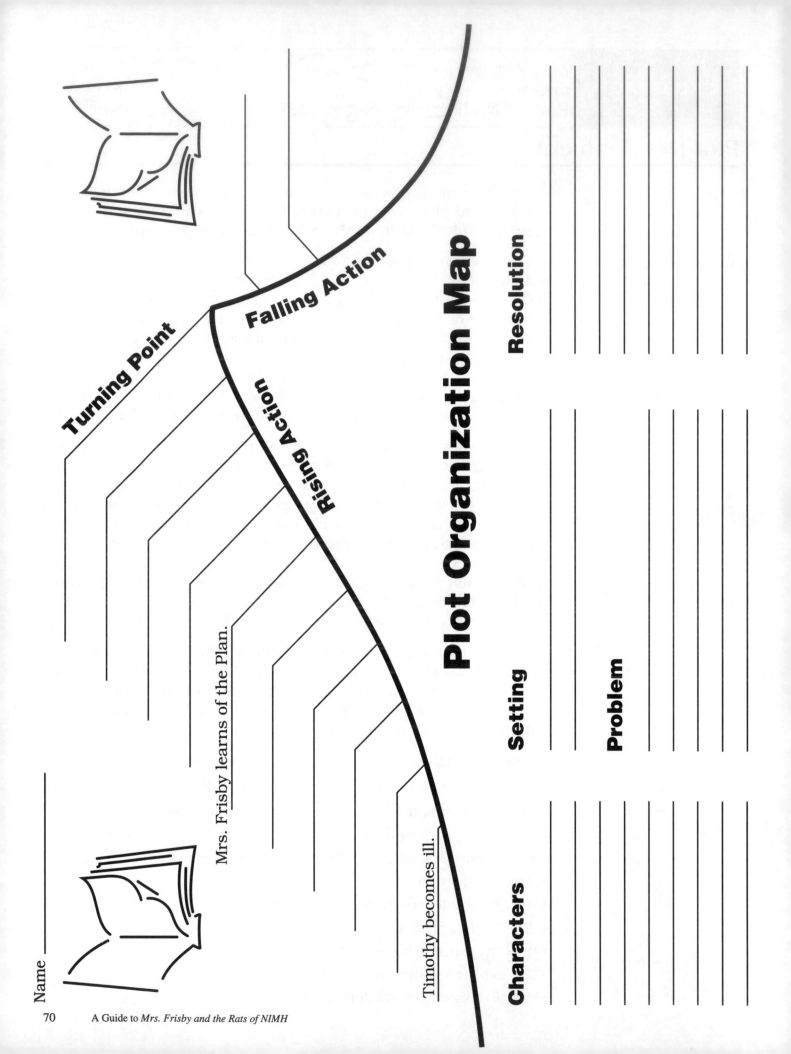

Plot Organization Map

Turning Point

Falling Action

Rising Action

Mrs. Frisby learns of the Plan.

Timothy becomes ill.

Resolution

Setting

Problem

Characters

Name _____

Name _____

Multiple Choice

Directions:

Circle the letter of the

correct answer.

1. On the morning after her adventure in the Fitzgibbons' kitchen, Mrs. Frisby was awakened by...

    A. her children.

    B. Justin.

    C. Brutus.

2. When the rats thought that the exterminators might be from NIMH, they were...

    A. curious because they wanted to see Dr. Schultz again.

    B. afraid because the NIMH scientists knew about their super-intelligence.

    C. happy because they knew the scientists wouldn't harm them.

3. The six or seven rats at Henderson's hardware store had probably...

    A. plugged in the motors to see if they worked properly.

    B. not been very smart.

    C. been electrocuted accidentally.

4. The rats planned that when the exterminators would bull-doze their storage room, they would find...

    A. a load of foul-smelling garbage.

    B. a room full of motors and books.

    C. ten rats of the rear guard.

5. The rats that volunteered for the rear guard knew that they...

    A. would surely be killed by the gas.

    B. would be captured by the scientists.

    C. would have a chance to escape from the hidden hole.

6. When Mrs. Frisby heard the tractor start up after the rats had escaped, she...

    A. knew her home was safe due to the rats' wise planning.

    B. knew that her cinder block would be destroyed.

    C. was preparing to move.

TEST

Mrs. Frisby
and the
Rats of NIMH

Chapters 26-28, Page 2

Name _____

7. The scientists, seeing the rats of the rear guard running in hectic fashion,...

    A. thought the rats were reacting to the gas.

    B. thought the rats were trying to bite them.

    C. were fooled into thinking there were many rats.

8. When Mrs. Frisby found the eighth rat who had emerged from the hole, she saw that it was...

    A. Justin.

    B. Nicodemus.

    C. Brutus.

9. When Mrs. Frisby saw her friend Janice at their summer home, she...

    A. told her about the rats and NIMH.

    B. kept the secret about the rats' identity.

    C. invited Janice into her home.

10. The Frisbys hoped to contact Jeremy again by...

    A. leaving something shiny out in the sun.

    B. sending him a message through the owl.

    C. asking Mr. Ages to contact him.

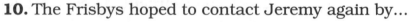

Vocabulary

Directions:

Fill in the blank with

the correct word.

presumed	donned	harrow
cryptically	antidote	deliberation
inexorable	frenzy	incredulously

1. _____ violent agitation; wild excitement

2. _____ unstoppable; unalterable

3. _____ a medicine or remedy for counteracting the effects of poison

4. _____   took for granted; supposed

5. _____   put on

6. _____   in a secretive manner

7. _____   farm implement used to level
                                   plowed land

8. _____   in an unbelieving manner

9. _____   careful consideration before a
                                   decision

Essay Questions

Directions:

Answer in complete

sentences.

1. The newspaper article about the rats found in Henderson's
   hardware store read: "Mechanized Rats Invade Hardware
   Store." At first, the rats were confused by this headline, but
   they later figured it out. Explain what the headline meant.

   _____

   _____

   _____

2. When the rats learned that they needed to leave Fitzgibbon's
   farm immediately, they weren't too alarmed. Why weren't the
   rats more concerned?

   _____

   _____

   _____

3. Nicodemus said that a rear guard of ten rats was essential for
   the rats' escape plan. Why did the rats need some rats to stay
   behind?

   _____

   _____

   _____

Chapter Title _____ Name _____

Chapter Summary: _____

_____

_____

_____

_____

_____

_____

_____

_____

_____

_____

_____

_____

_____

_____

_____

Chapter Vocabulary:

1. _____

_____

2. _____

_____

3. _____

_____

4. _____

_____

NAME: _____

Mrs. Frisby and the Rats of NIMH

Skill Page: Writing About Fantasy. Page 11.

1. C
2. E
3. G
4. A
5. D
6. B
7. F

Test: Chapters 1-5. Pages 14-16.

Multiple Choice

1.	B	6.	A
2.	C	7.	C
3.	B	8.	B
4.	B	9.	C
5.	C	10.	B

Vocabulary

1. subdued	6. apt
2. dubiously	7. vigorous
3. relentlessly	8. illogical
4. respite	9. tedious
5. hypochondriac	10. laboriously

Essay Questions

1. Timothy kept others happy by joking with them. He was always kind even to his scatter brained sister, Cynthia, and he never lost patience with her. When she lost things, he would help her find them. When she was sick, he would entertain her. P. 21.

2. This statement means that just because someone has a large head doesn't necessarily mean that the person has a lot of brains. Jeremy had a large head, but he wasn't very smart. P. 24.

3. Mrs. Frisby couldn't move Timothy because he was recovering from pneumonia and was supposed to stay in bed. If Timothy got cold, he might never recover. To move to their summer home meant a long walk across the field of winter wheat, and the home itself would be damp and chilly for the first few weeks. P. 30.

Accept reasonable answers.

Skill Page: Elements of a Narrative. Page 22.

Main Character

A. Mrs. Frisby was responsible. She took good care of her family, keeping a cozy home for them. She was always looking for better food to feed her family.

B. Mrs. Frisby was cheerful. Even though her husband was dead, Mrs. Frisby always looked on the bright side of things.

C. Mrs. Frisby was careful. She kept a constant lookout for dangerous animals, like the cat.

Setting

A. Where: Mr. Fitzgibbon's vegetable garden.

B. When: Present time.

Plot

A. Mrs. Frisby, a widowed mouse with four children, seeks help for her sick son, Timothy, from Mr. Ages.

B. Mrs. Frisby helps untangle Jeremy, a crow caught on a fence by some silver string.

C. Mrs. Frisby learns that she must move before Timothy will be well.

D. Jeremy advises Mrs. Frisby to seek help from the owl about Moving Day.

E. The owl advises Mrs. Frisby to ask help from an unusual group of rats, who have sworn the owl to secrecy.

Accept reasonable answers.

Skill Sheet: About the Characters. Page 24.

A widow mouse who had four young children — Mrs. Frisby

An old, wise white mouse who knew about medicine — Mr. Ages

Youngest, scatter brained child of Mrs. Frisby — Cynthia

A large, young, muscular rat who guarded the rats' home — Brutus

Mrs. Frisby's handsome, strong son — Martin

A wise old bird who gave advice to other birds — the owl

An older rat who guarded the rats' home — Justin

A crow who collected bright shiny objects — Jeremy

Mr. Fitzgibbon's ferocious cat — Dragon

Mrs. Frisby's frailest, most thoughtful child — Timothy

Small animal friend of Mrs. Frisby — the shrew

The farmer on whose farm Mrs. Frisby lived — Mr. Fitzgibbon

Mrs. Frisby's responsible, older daughter — Theresa

Mrs. Frisby's well-respected, deceased husband — Jonathan Frisby

Skill Page: Sequencing. Page 30.

Event 1:   Timothy Frisby becomes ill.

Event 2:   Mr. Ages prescribes medicine.

Event 3:   Mrs. Frisby helps Jeremy.

Event 4:   Mr. Fitzgibbon prepares to plow.

Event 5:   Mrs. Frisby sees rats marching.

Event 6:   Mrs. Frisby asks the owl for help.

Event 7:   Owl learns Mrs. Frisby's identity.

Event 8:   Mrs. Frisby goes to the rats' rosebush.

Event 9:   Brutus sends Mrs. Frisby away.

Event 10: Mrs. Frisby meets Justin.

Event 11: Mrs. Frisby is introduced to Nicodemus.

Event 12: Mrs. Frisby wonders about the Plan.

Test: Chapters 6-10. Pages 25-27.

Multiple Choice

1. C		6. C	
2. B		7. B	
3. B		8. A	
4. C		9. C	
5. A		10. C	

Vocabulary

1. feasible	6. agitated
2. cordial	7. timidly
3. domain	8. expedition
4. perceive	9. doubtful
5. plummeted	10. sentry

Essay Questions

1. Jonathan Frisby, Mrs. Frisby's deceased husband, had been highly respected by both the owl and the rats. P. 55-56, 58, 73.

2. Timothy was frail and sickly. Martin liked danger and excitement. When Martin saw Jeremy the crow, he wished that he could ride on the crow's back. P. 46.

   Accept reasonable answers.

Skill Page: Cause and Effect. Page 33.

1. D	6. A
2. G	7. E
3. C	8. I
4. J	9. F
5. B	10. H

Test: Chapters 11-15. Pages 35-37.

Multiple Choice

1. B	6. B
2. C	7. A
3. C	8. C
4. A	9. C
5. B	10. C

Vocabulary

1. scrutiny	6. cowered
2. futile	7. recounted
3. contritely	8. hostile
4. detect	9. converged
5. explicit	10. irrelevantly

Essay Questions

1. Mr. Ages made a sleeping powder to slip into Dragon's food to make him drowsy. To accomplish this, a small mouse (the rats were too large) had to crawl through a hole in the kitchen floor behind the cabinet where Dragon's dish was kept.

2. Jonathan Frisby had died trying to help the rats by slipping sleeping powder into Dragon's food.

3. Dr. Schultz put the sixty-three rats into three groups. Twenty rats were in each of groups A and B. Twenty-three were in group C. Groups A and B were given injections twice a week. Group C wasn't given injections; they were merely stuck with needles. The rats at first had no idea about the nature of the experiment.

Accept reasonable answers.

Skill Page: About the Lab at NIMH. Page 40.

•Lab Input•

	Group A-Rats	Group B-Rats	Group C-Rats	Group G-Mice
Number in Group	20 rats	20 rrats	23 rats	8 mice
Food Type	scientific pellets	scientific pellets	scientific pellets	scientific pellets
Living Conditions	cages	cages	cages	cages
Testing Methods	mazes/shape recognition	mazes/shape recognition	mazes/shape recognition	mazes/shape recognition
DNA Injections	strong dosage	weak dosage	no dosage	strong dosage
Steroid Injections	strong dosage	weak dosage	no dosage	strong dosage
Injection Frequency	twice a week	twice a week	none	twice a week

•Lab Outcome•

	Group A-Rats	Group B-Rats	Group C-Rats	Group G-Mice
Learning Speed	300% ahead of group C	20% ahead of group C	no change	300% ahead of group C
Stimulus Reactions	300% ahead of group C	20% ahead of group C	no change	300% ahead of group C
Longevity	more than double lifespan	no change	no change	more than double lifespan

Skill Page: About the Characters, Prt 2. Page 45.

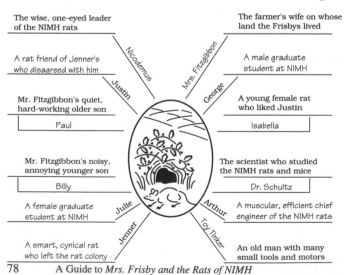

The wise, one-eyed leader of the NIMH rats — Nicodemus

The farmer's wife on whose land the Frisbys lived — Mrs. Fitzgibbon

A rat friend of Jenner's who disagreed with him — Justin

A male graduate student at NIMH — George

Mr. Fitzgibbon's quiet, hard-working older son — Paul

A young female rat who liked Justin — Isabella

Mr. Fitzgibbon's noisy, annoying younger son — Billy

The scientist who studied the NIMH rats and mice — Dr. Schultz

A female graduate student at NIMH — Julie

A muscular, efficient chief engineer of the NIMH rats — Arthur

A smart, cynical rat who left the rat colony — Jenner

An old man with many small tools and motors — Toy Tinker

Test: Chapters 16-20. Pages 46-48.

Multiple Choice

1. C	6. A
2. B	7. B
3. C	8. B
4. A	9. C
5. C	10. B

Vocabulary

1. cursory	6. ritual
2. plaintive	7. skeptical
3. illusion	8. astute
4. discontent	9. strode
5. portal	10. submitted

Essay Questions

1. The entire building at NIMH was air conditioned, so the rats couldn't escape through an open window. The air ducts led to a main air shaft, which led to the outside and freedom.

2. Before exploring the air ducts to find the main air shaft, the rats worried that they would lose their way back. The rats used the thread like a rope to feel their way back in the dark. They used the screwdriver to anchor the spool of thread. On their escape night, the mice used the screwdriver to pry open the wire screen that separated them from the outside.

3. Jenner knew that the NIMH rats were much smarter than other rats, so they might not be accepted into other rat colonies. He also thought that the NIMH rats might be disgusted with stealing their food, eating from garbage cans, and living in sewers, as they had done before their stay at NIMH.

Accept reasonable answers.

Skill Page: Outlining. Page 52.

The Plan

I. The Rats' Main Hall

   A. Description

      1. Large, bright room

      2. Filled with working rats

   B. Size—almost 20 feet square

   C. History

      1. Natural cave

      2. Used in the past

II. The Rats' Plow
   A. Design
      1. By Nicodemus
      2. Small and light
      3. Pulled by 8 rats
   B. Usefulness
      1. Plow earth
      2. Grow own food
III. Storage Bins
   A. Grains
      1. Types
         a. Barley
         b. Corn
         c. Soy beans
      2. Quantities
         a. 2-year supply
         b. Feed 108 rats
   B. Fruit and Vegetable Seeds
IV. Plan's Purpose
   A. Build rat civilization
   B. Live without stealing
V. Thorn Valley
   A. Location of new home
   B. Advice from owl
   C. Beautiful, safe spot

Test: Chapters 21-25. Pages 60-62.

Multiple Choice

1.	B	6.	C
2.	A	7.	B
3.	C	8.	C
4.	B	9.	B
5.	C	10.	C

Vocabulary

1.	admonished	6.	defiant
2.	defective	7.	scavengers
3.	heirs	8.	solitude
4.	cynical	9.	pessimist
5.	reluctant	10.	retreated

Essay Questions

1. In order to build a rat civilization, the rats would have to develop their own art, science, religion, and government and not merely copy humans' civilization. The rats would have to give up their easy life of stealing food, electric power, and water. They would need to grow their own food and work harder without motors.

2. Jenner was more cynical than the other rats. He saw nothing wrong with stealing. He felt that the NIMH rats were much smarter than other beings, and he figured he could always outwit anyone attempting to get in his way. Jenner never believed the rats would be successful in building a new civilization. Nicodemus, on the other hand, never felt the rats had a civilization on the farm. He felt that they were just piggy-backing on the humans' civilization. He wasn't sure the Plan would work, but he and the others wanted to try.

3. The Public Health Service had heard about the rats from the newspaper article reporting the incident at the hardware store. The federal government wanted to exterminate all area rats with cyanide gas. The article claimed that a doctor would check in town on the following day, and that he would bring in a bull-dozer to destroy the rosebush by the rats' colony.

Accept reasonable answers.

Skill Page: Character Development. Page 66.

Jenner	Nicodemus
Responsibility	**Responsibility**
1. Liked easy life of stealing. Thought that because he was smart, he could handle anything.	1. Wanted rats to be independent. Wanted to build a rat civilization.
Courage	**Courage**
1. Brave—escaped from cage at NIMH.	1. Brave—escaped from cage at NIMH.
2. Left rat colony to go out on his own with 6 other rats.	2. Took risks even when Dragon was on the prowl.
Compassion	**Compassion**
1. Did not care about others' feelings.	1. Agreed to help Mrs. Frisby with her Moving Day problem.
Loyalty	**Loyalty**
1. Helped rats escape NIMH.	1. Helped rats escape NIMH.
2. Not loyal to his rat colony.	2. Led his rats well.
	3. Helped Mrs. Frisby because her late husband was the rats' friend.
Honesty	**Honesty**
1. Stealing didn't bother him.	1. Wanted to build a rat civilization where rats could provide for themselves.
Friendship	**Friendship**
1. Deserted his old friend Nicodemus.	1. Became friends with Justin at NIMH. They both freed all the other rats.
	2. Helped Jonathan escape from NIMH.

3. Became friends with the owl.
4. Helped Mrs. Frisby with Moving Day.

Persistence
1. Wanted a quick, easy way of life.

Persistence
1. Spent one year developing the Plan. Took three years to learn how to farm, collect grains and seeds, and build equipment needed.

Hard Work
1. Did not mind hard work.
2. Gave advice to rats about escape from NIMH.

Self-discipline
1. Liked the easy life.

Hard Work
1. Worked at helping rats escape from NIMH.
2. Worked for three years to prepare for move to Thorn Valley.
3. Developed plow to use to grow food.

Self-discipline
1. Worked toward greater goals in the long run.

Accept reasonable answers

Skill Page: Plot Structure. Page 69.

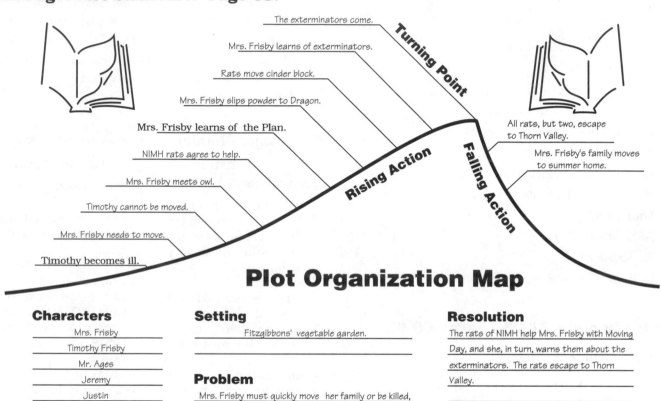

The exterminators come.

Mrs. Frisby learns of exterminators.

Rats move cinder block.

Mrs. Frisby slips powder to Dragon.

Mrs. Frisby learns of the Plan.

NIMH rats agree to help.

Mrs. Frisby meets owl.

Timothy cannot be moved.

Mrs. Frisby needs to move.

Timothy becomes ill.

Turning Point

Rising Action

Falling Action

All rats, but two, escape to Thorn Valley.

Mrs. Frisby's family moves to summer home.

Plot Organization Map

Characters
Mrs. Frisby
Timothy Frisby
Mr. Ages
Jeremy
Justin
Nicodemus
Mr. Fitzgibbon
Dr. Schultz

Setting
Fitzgibbons' vegetable garden.

Problem
Mrs. Frisby must quickly move her family or be killed, but her sick son, Timothy, cannot be moved. Mrs. Frisby learns that her friends, the NIMH rats, must also move or be exterminated.

Resolution
The rats of NIMH help Mrs. Frisby with Moving Day, and she, in turn, warns them about the exterminators. The rats escape to Thorn Valley.

Test: Chapters 26-28. Page 71-73.

Multiple Choice

1. C
2. B
3. C
4. A
5. C

6. A
7. C
8. C
9. B
10. A

Vocabulary

1. frenzy
2. inexorable
3. antidote
4. presumed
5. donned

6. cryptically
7. harrow
8. incredulously
9. deliberation

Essay Questions

1. The headline meant that someone thought the rats knew about electricity and how to use motors. Nicodemus, and others, assumed Jenner's group had probably stolen motors or tools, which would have made them seem mechanized.

2. The rats already had a great deal of food and seeds at Thorn Valley. With luck they would have a first crop by fall.

3. The rats needed a rear guard to stay behind because if the exterminators found an empty rat hole, they would have been suspicious.